Customer Care

A training manual for library staff

PAT GANNON-LEARY
AND
MICHAEL D. MCCARTHY

Chandos Publishing

Oxford • Cambridge • New Delhi

Chandos Publishing
TBAC Business Centre
Avenue 4
Station Lane
Witney
Oxford OX28 4BN
UK
Tel: +44 (0) 1993 848726
Email: info@chandospublishing.com
www.chandospublishing.com

Chandos Publishing is an imprint of Woodhead Publishing Limited

Woodhead Publishing Limited
Abington Hall
Granta Park
Great Abington
Cambridge CB21 6AH
UK
www.woodheadpublishing.com

First published in 2010

ISBN:
978 1 84334 570 1

© P. Gannon-Leary and M. D. McCarthy, 2010

Typeset by Domex e-Data Pvt. Ltd.
Printed in the UK and USA.

Customer Care

CHANDOS
INFORMATION PROFESSIONAL SERIES

Series Editor: Ruth Rikowski
(email: Rikowskigr@aol.com)

Chandos' new series of books are aimed at the busy information professional. They have been specially commissioned to provide the reader with an authoritative view of current thinking. They are designed to provide easy-to-read and (most importantly) practical coverage of topics that are of interest to librarians and other information professionals. If you would like a full listing of current and forthcoming titles, please visit our website www.chandospublishing.com or email info@chandospublishing.com or telephone +44 (0) 1223 891358.

New authors: we are always pleased to receive ideas for new titles; if you would like to write a book for Chandos, please contact Dr Glyn Jones on email gjones@chandospublishing.com or telephone number +44 (0) 1993 848726.

Bulk orders: some organisations buy a number of copies of our books. If you are interested in doing this, we would be pleased to discuss a discount. Please email info@chandospublishing.com or telephone +44 (0) 1223 891358.

Contents

List of figures and tables

Figures

Tables

About the authors

Pat Gannon-Leary is a consultant and joint partner of Bede Research & Consultancy with Michael D. McCarthy. Dr Gannon-Leary was previously a researcher at the universities of Northumbria and Newcastle. Her earlier career experience includes a variety of roles in academic libraries in the UK and the USA, including as a customer service manager. During that time she facilitated customer care courses for library staff. She has taught research methods and has a special interest in focus groups, which she used as an information practitioner to determine library user needs. She is co-author of *Providing Effective Library Services for Research* (London: Facet Press, 2007) and, along with one of her co-authors (Moira Bent) has recently been running workshops on supporting researchers who are writing for publication. She has been published widely and has presented at conferences in the UK and overseas.

Michael D. McCarthy served as a senior officer in the logistics branch of the RAF, including three years as a specialist instructor to officer cadets. During his RAF service he was active in mountain rescue, and for many years led expeditions to the Bavarian and Austrian Alps. On leaving the RAF, he moved into the management of customer support in major aerospace companies in the UK and Sweden. He has wide experience of customer support activity throughout the European aerospace community, covering both major contractors and suppliers. Following early retirement, he has recently spent two years working in a support role in a university library in order to obtain 'hands-on' experience of the demands of customer care in this particular environment.

The authors may be contacted at:

Bede Research & Consultancy
97 Westfield
Windy Nook
Gateshead, NE10 8PD
UK

E-mail: *pgleary@aol.com* and *michael.d.mccarthy@blueyonder.co.uk*

Acknowledgments

The authors would like to thank the following:

- Adam Murray of Murray State University
- Ali Pickard of Northumbria University
- Alison Wallace of Thomas Cook
- Celia Wall of Murray State University
- Fiona MacDonald of Christchurch Polytechnic Institute of Technology
- Janice Goldie of Dumfries and Galloway Libraries
- Jill Beard of Bournemouth University
- June Schmidt of Mississippi Libraries
- Kelly Czarnecki of the Public Library of Charlotte & Mecklenburg County
- Lynn Barrett of the University of Huddersfield
- Margie Jantti of the University of Wollongong
- Mary Jane Rootes of the University of West Georgia
- Moira Bent of Newcastle University
- Nicola Horsey of Hampshire Libraries
- Rolf Hapel of Aarhus Library
- Steve Backs of Monroe County Public Library

Preface

The overarching aim of this manual and the associated programme is to help people to develop both communication and quality service skills in order to deliver best practice support to their customers and to their colleagues.

By investing in this manual and in encouraging staff to develop as facilitators, your organisation is acknowledging the vital role of your staff in successfully achieving your organisational mission.

Members of your organisation form a community of diverse people working together for a common purpose. You may be an educational institution, you may be in the public sector, or you may be in the voluntary sector. Wherever you are, you will no doubt wish to give your customers the same 'best practice' quality service that commercial, non-academic businesses are expected to deliver to their clients.

In order to achieve their aims, the manual and the programme have set a number of objectives:

- to clarify what is meant by 'customer service';
- to heighten awareness of customers' needs;
- to develop staff communication skills;
- to develop skills that enable staff to meet their responsibilities with less stress, e.g. dealing with complaints, handling difficult customers;
- to help increase staff awareness of their own importance and of their performance in contributing to the delivery of the organisational mission.

The customer care course should give participants insight into methods that enable them to communicate more positively with colleagues and with customers, and thereby enjoy more positive relationships with those groups. Being engaged in more positive interaction is likely to enhance staff job satisfaction significantly and, in turn, help improve staff performance. Staff subjected to lower levels of stress will find their jobs more personally rewarding, in addition to feeling better about themselves and their role in the organisation.

We can all give examples of poor quality service. Indeed, one of the exercises in this manual involves identifying such examples. Poor quality service tends to happen when the people delivering it fail to put a high value on their work, don't experience satisfaction in a job well done, and take no pride in their work.

We can all, hopefully, give some examples of good quality service too. Again there is an exercise in the manual to identify such examples. Successful people perform their jobs to the best of their abilities, setting high standards and meeting them – or even exceeding them. When staff take pride in their achievement and have positive feelings about themselves, this can have an invaluable, beneficial knock-on effect on those around them – both colleagues and customers – and can make them feel good too.

This training manual is based on our experience as customer service and customer support managers, and our experience of staff training and development in customer service programmes. Our aim throughout has been to present information in a user-friendly fashion, so that your confidence in presenting its contents increases as you read through it and become more comfortable and familiar with it. Please take time to browse through it and get a feel for what we are aiming to do here.

We hope you find its structure logical yet flexible. It is designed to be used as both a reference book and/or as a training manual. It may be used by staff in human resources or staff development areas to organise and then facilitate their own tailored programmes. At the same time, it is designed to encourage the delivery of training by non-specialist, non-professional trainers from across the departmental spectrum.

We hope you find it straightforward and easy to use. We have not assumed that you have a de luxe training room or numerous electronic bells and whistles. We are also aware that you may not have a great deal of time to spend in preparing materials to use with the group(s). On this basis we have tried to 'keep it simple' as regards the training aids and props you will need in order to deliver the course.

Anyone wishing to run focus groups related to customer service issues will be able to 'cherry-pick' useful items or excerpts from the manual, as it has been specifically written with this in mind. For those who are new to focus groups, Chapter 10 covers these in more depth and also provides some useful further reading.

The book is suited for both one and two-day courses. There are enough exercises and options for facilitators to 'pick and mix' to fit their available timeslot, and to ensure that they choose those options with which they are personally comfortable. Course facilitators will need sufficient time to read through the content of this manual and decide which activities they wish to include. They will also require some lead time to convert relevant resources from the manual into forms better suited for the participants.

The following timetable demonstrates how the chapter sessions could be fitted into a two-day course:

- Day 1:
  - Chapter 2 – Introduction (45 minutes)
  - Coffee (chance to get to know each other better, talk over feelings about doing the course etc.)
  - Chapter 3 – What is customer service? (30 minutes)
  - Chapter 4 – Who are our customers? (50 minutes)
  - Lunch (chance to talk about course so far, your customers and their needs)
  - Chapter 5 – Communication (50 minutes)
  - Chapter 6 – Questioning and active listening (45 minutes)
  - Tea (chance to talk over progress of course, listening exercises)
  - Chapter 7 – Handling complaints (70 minutes)
  - End of Day 1

- Day 2:
  - Chapter 8 – Dealing with challenging situations (60 minutes)
  - Coffee (chance to talk over yesterday)
  - Chapter 9 – OK Corral and life positions (70 minutes)
  - Lunch (chance to talk about customer service situations, influencing styles)
  - Chapter 10 – Suggestions for improvement (70 minutes)
  - Chapter 11 – Teambuilding (40+ minutes)
  - Tea (useful recap of course before final session and before feedback forms)
  - Chapter 12 – What are we good at? (70 minutes)
  - Chapter 13 – Wrapping it up (20 minutes)

You will note that the sum total for each day's activities is approximately five hours per day, excluding, say, a further 90 minutes for lunch and coffee breaks. We have planned this slight shortfall in the normal working day in order to cater for the tendency of inexperienced or unfamiliar facilitators to run slightly over time in their initial efforts to present a course such as this. At this early stage, we cannot overemphasise the central importance of time management in the successful delivery of training. If you allow the timetable to 'get away from you' in the early stages, you will then be constantly struggling to get back on track, so it's best not to go there in the first place.

For preference, courses should be limited to 8–12 participants, although limited resources may demand larger groups. A maximum of 25–30 would be advisable. These staff should ideally come from a variety of levels and locations, but the groups should have sufficient in common for facilitators to pitch the presentation at an appropriate level and create a more productive synergy. Where possible, it may be helpful to mix staff that have not previously worked together. For such circumstances, this manual includes suggested 'icebreakers' as a means of improving both communication and interaction.

The manual follows the order in which sessions are run. For each session there are details of the aims and a tabular session plan giving an outline of the activities, materials and time needed to complete the session. Times are approximate because, in many cases, facilitators have a choice of activities within each session. They can use those they feel most comfortable with and that they feel are most appropriate for their particular group of participants. In addition, many chapters have exemplars of best practice and case studies which can be used to supplement activities or as discussion points.

Content marked 'background' is descriptive in nature, outlining the nature of the issue being discussed. Facilitators may want to make a few notes from this area to use during the course, or to serve as an aide memoire. The text in this section will form the basis of the brief introductory talk for each session given by facilitators, marked as 'T' on the session plans (Table 0.1 presents a blank session plan template – feel free to adapt this to use in your preparation). In addition to activities ('A' on the session plan), there are accompanying handouts. You may wish to copy or scan these but, in some cases, it is probably easier to write up flipcharts.

Good luck in running the course(s) and in developing your own facilitation skills and confidence via our structured, low-risk training and learning process.

Please let us know how you got on. We value your feedback and we too are seeking to continuously improve.

Pat Gannon-Leary and Michael D. McCarthy

Table 0.1 Session plan template

Session title	Aims	Content	Methods*	Aids*	Time (mins)
Approx. total time (mins)					

*A, activity (participants); F/C, flipchart; H/O, handout; P/I, Post-it notes; T, talk (facilitator)

Preparation

Prepare and prevent, rather than repair and repent. (Anon)

When you're thirsty, it's too late to think about digging a well. (Anon)

Your role as a facilitator

In your role as facilitator, you will be using your skills, instinct and experience to decide when and where you might need to intervene in the training process. You have the background materials you need and we have given advice about the additional props to use, but there is no 'script' to which you must rigidly adhere as you will be required to respond to the developing situation.

You will know what you and the participants are hoping to get from the course, and rest assured you are not expected to be an expert in the subject of 'customer care' – this is not a prerequisite. The participants are bringing their own experiences of customer care to the course and you are helping them to elicit these experiences, to share them with others and to reflect on lessons learned.

Course facilitators can be taken from staff from across the departmental spectrum. We recommend that inexperienced staff operate in pairs. Three or four hours is a long time for one person to talk, and it is also a long time for participants to listen to a single voice. By dividing up the responsibilities for the various sessions of the course (with the other facilitator free to interject comments at any time or to step in if their partner dries up), you should keep both the participants and facilitator from tiring and keep the course running smoothly.

Depending on the size of the organisation, you may want to have a core team of facilitators who work in pairs, but mix up the pairings so that everyone works with everyone else in the core team. Experience has shown us that this works particularly well, as facilitators learn from each other and everyone brings their own unique style to the programme. This may not be feasible in a smaller organisation, so you may want to consider working with another organisation to pool resources, and bring facilitators and participants from both organisations together. For example, we once facilitated for a mixed group of university library staff and public library staff from the same city. This can result in a valuable exchange of experience.

To facilitate successfully, your first responsibility is to keep the group on task. Second, having established the ground rules for the course (see below), you need to ensure that participants stick to what has been agreed. Finally, you must ensure that the participants understand what they are being asked to do and that you are not asking them to step too far outside their comfort zone.

Adult learning theory emphasises that adults are self-directed and learn from connecting their personal experiences to new knowledge. A climate of mutual trust and positive reinforcement to enhance learning is a critical component of this theory.

The facilitator should bear in mind the following characteristics and needs of adult learners:

- they are usually highly motivated;
- their time is limited because of their many other responsibilities;
- they want to leave the learning situation with something significant;
- they bring to the course a wealth of resources – knowledge, experience, skills and practised intellectual ability.

With these characteristics in mind, the courses should be structured around the participants responding individually to the issues raised or questions posed, or discussing issues in groups, which can range in size from two to the whole group, with a rapporteur presenting the collective response either orally or on a flipchart or whiteboard. Given that the facilitator may be conducting the course alone, it may be worth getting each group of participants to appoint a chair and a rapporteur. The former ensures that the group stays focused on the topic; the latter takes notes and is prepared to make a presentation based on the group's responses. This format should be followed throughout the duration of the course, but chairs and rapporteurs should change for each activity so that all participants have the opportunity to fulfil both roles.

Notes on venue and facilities

The venue must be large enough to seat all the participants in groups of three to six in moveable chairs with moveable tables facing a screen and a flipchart on a stand (not necessarily all in position at the same time). Tables can impose a barrier between facilitator and participants so are best used for the breakaway sessions. If the room is large enough for the inclusion of tables, this can obviate the need for separate breakaway rooms.

We have assumed you will have access to a flipchart and stand and possibly also a whiteboard or similar. You may have a PC on which you can project scanned documents onto a pull-down wall screen or whiteboard. Do not worry if this is not the case – you can scan or photocopy the handouts from the book and write other text on the flipchart – it just means a little more advance preparation on your part.

While the session plans refer to the use of flipcharts (F/C), you don't necessarily need to use these. If there is a whiteboard, you might wish to make use of this – in which case, ensure you have the right type of pens available. One possible alternative to the flipchart is to give participants pads of Post-it® notes and get them to make a 'graffiti wall' of their responses on the Post-it® notes. There are various sizes of Post-it® note, so get a size large enough for people to write on comfortably. Genius Pads™ for example are 30 cm × 30 cm (11.81 in × 11.81 in) and come in a stack of 80 sheets. If you do decide to create a graffiti wall, then do first ensure that this will not damage your venue's walls. If in doubt, use windows or unpainted woodwork to form the graffiti wall. If the venue has a cabaret-style layout with participants sitting around tables, you might prefer another alternative to the flipchart – the use of white paper tablecloths on which participants write their comments and then shout them from the floor. This style of interactivity is sometimes known as a 'learning café'.

If you are writing on the flipchart, make sure the text is sufficiently large for the participants to read. Lettering should be simple, bold and colourful. Similarly, if you are projecting documents onto a screen, test out the font sizes beforehand in the room where the training is to be held. Participants will be frustrated and distracted if they can't see things clearly.

Flipcharts are useful for building up simple visual messages which can be revealed in stages, but they do interrupt eye contact/rapport between facilitator and participants. If there are two facilitators, this issue can be overcome if one is writing while the other is talking and maintaining rapport. If you are facilitating solo, try not to write and talk at the same time. You may wish to prepare some flipcharts in advance, in which case, check your familiarity with the sequence beforehand so that you know what to expect.

Check that you know how to use any technology that you are going to employ, such as remote control devices. In addition, if you are taking your own laptop to an external venue and anticipating linking it to their presentation technology, check in advance that your software is compatible with theirs. Again for external venues, it is also a good idea to have a backup plan in case of a catastrophic failure of either their or even your own technology. Emergency handouts, ready-made flipcharts and even overhead projector slides can be an invaluable insurance policy against IT failure.

Ensure the correct positioning of laptops etc. so that you can operate them and read your notes without obstructing the participants' view. Check the lighting in the training room is sufficiently bright for you to be able to read your notes but sufficiently dark for participants to be able to read the screen.

With respect to stationery, ensure you have:

- enough copy paper for the handouts;
- flipchart(s);
- different-coloured pens/highlighters suitable for use on flipcharts;
- Blu-Tack® (to stick flipcharts onto boards/walls);
- card (folded) to act as name plates/badges/sticky labels;
- Genius Pads™/Post-it® notes;
- white paper table cloths for the learning café approach – if you have tables.

The introduction

We naturally admire the wisdom and good judgment of those who come to us for advice... (Anon)

An intelligent person not only knows how to accept advice, but also how to reject it. (Anon)

Aims

The aims of the introduction are as follows:

- to introduce course members and facilitator(s);
- to express any concerns about the course, and create a climate for learning;
- to understand the aims and structure of the customer care programme;
- to establish ground rules;
- to clarify the role of the facilitator(s).

Background

This chapter covers the introduction to the course and, as such, contains some detailed notes for facilitators. Please don't be put off by this – later chapters are more straightforward!

As with all courses, at the outset the facilitator will need to introduce themselves (and their partner if they are working in a pair), expressing the hope that the participants will enjoy the course. They also may need to issue a set of housekeeping directions, such as identifying the location of the cloakrooms and toilets, where (and when) refreshments are available, and what to do in case of a fire.

Remember that the tone of a course can be set by the way it is opened. In introducing the course, the facilitator(s) should:

- explain that they hope everyone will work together to harness the wealth of resources in the room – the knowledge, experience, skills and intellectual capacity of the participants;
- reiterate that sessions are intended to be interactive.

A key responsibility of the facilitator(s) is to provide a non-threatening environment conducive to active participation and sharing. It is also important that they be flexible and adaptable as the interactive nature of the sessions will make it very difficult to stick precisely to the prepared material. Here it is worth recalling our previous comments about time-keeping. Should you at any time feel that the participants' questions or comments are likely to get you off track, it is sensible to use a 'parking lot' to store these issues; for example, you might write them on a flipchart to be picked up later as/when/if they become appropriate.

It is important to engage the participants. Tips for this include:

- make eye contact with all participants – don't miss out sections of the room;
- move around the space to include all participants in the discussion;
- encourage people to ask questions if they would like to – aim for experience sharing;
- capture expectations and check with participants during the course that these are being addressed;
- if expectations are not being addressed, try to be flexible with your agenda;
- be aware of the interest of the participants and of their level of concentration – if you sense they need a break, give them one;
- don't speak in a monotone;
- if appropriate, use energisers to revitalise participants (see below);
- keep points clear and concise;
- ensure participants have time to absorb information – use pauses where appropriate to allow this to happen;
- relax and enjoy yourself.

Aim 1: Introductions

If the participants know each other, it might not be necessary to make introductions. Even if they are known to each other, they may not be known to the facilitators, so you may want to go round the group asking for names. There are various ways of doing this, and it is for the facilitator to decide how comfortable they feel with the different methods. Perhaps the most formal method would be to go around and ask for names, departments/service and roles. In addition, you could ask people why they are there today, or what they hope to get from the course.

At this stage, nerves may limit participants' memories, so it is worth writing these points on a flipchart in the form a bullet list, thus:

- name;
- work department/section/team;
- job title;
- what you hope to learn/achieve by your participation here.

The first three bullets remind the participants what they are being asked to say, and the facilitators can ask about the last point as they go round the group. By asking for a response to this last point, the facilitator has an opportunity to set expectations and align the participants. Participants' responses to the last point can be captured on the flipchart and revisited towards the end of the course to see if they have been met.

More informally, you can ask participants to start off by chatting for a couple of minutes to the person sitting next to them, then to introduce that person to the group. Another informal approach, in a group where everyone knows everybody else, might be to ask each person to say their name and one fact about themselves that other members of the group might not know.

Depending on the size of the group and how well the participants are known to the facilitator and to each other it may be desirable for them to write down their names and place of work on a firm piece of folded cardboard to serve as a nameplate. Alternatively, badges or sticky labels may be used by individual participants. If you prefer this option, then ask the participants to write in large, bold letters, otherwise the writing can be too small to read.

Icebreaker

Icebreakers normally form an important part of training events, as they can reduce the inhibitions of participants and enhance the enjoyment of a session. However, facilitators should give careful thought to a number of issues when preparing icebreakers.

The main area to consider is that the organisers of a training event have a 'duty of care' to participants, and need to take reasonable precautions to ensure their safety and wellbeing. Don't organise an icebreaker unless you are prepared to be responsible for that activity.

What is the purpose of the icebreaker?

There is no point introducing an icebreaker simply for the sake of it. Although icebreakers are good for reducing participants' inhibitions and enhancing their enjoyment, as the facilitator, you need to decide whether or not an icebreaker is appropriate to the circumstances. The purpose of an icebreaker could be some or all of the following:

- a means of making introductions;
- to help remember other participants' names;
- to get participants thinking about customer care/service;
- to find out why participants are attending.

The icebreaker should last no longer than ten minutes.

Who are the participants?

The main purpose is to make people feel comfortable and more relaxed about attending the customer care course, and to engage more readily in subsequent session activities. For this reason you should studiously avoid any kind of icebreaker with the potential to harm anyone either physically or emotionally.

Bear in mind that some participants may have 'hidden' special needs which may not be discernible to you or to other participants, but which could cause them both embarrassment and disadvantage them during the icebreaker.

There is also a need to recognise diversity among the participants. For example, icebreakers that involve touching another participant could be deemed inappropriate or even offensive by participants from some cultures.

Icebreakers that are overly competitive can also bring out the worst in people and have the potential to cause friction – not what you want at the outset of a course.

Practical guidance

Don't be put off by all the 'negative advice' above. The following comprises practical recommendations to help ensure that your icebreakers go smoothly, safely and enjoyably:

- Before the icebreaker, check that all participants are able to participate in the activity. On a confidential basis, offer them the chance to indicate any special needs or requirements that they have or need. This can be done by speaking to people individually or by prior notification. Any icebreaker or game that is discriminatory should be avoided.

- Make sure that the customer care session is a 'safe environment' by ensuring that participation in any activity is voluntary. Don't pressure people into doing something that they don't want to do.

- Check that any floors, props, and any other equipment are in a safe condition (i.e. no spillage, obstacles or other hazards).

- If an icebreaker or game consists of physical activity, warn people prior to the game of the need to be careful, and outline any possible risks.

- If you are in any doubt about particular icebreakers or games, do not try them, as the consequences could be far-reaching.

- If you need to get people into groups for icebreakers, one fun way of doing this is to use a pack of playing cards. You can shuffle these and distribute one to each person. You can then suggest, for example, that all the 'fours' get together, or all those of the same suit get together. Alternatively, depending on numbers, you can suggest that they make a 'run' or a 'flush' – assuming you all know your poker hands!

Suggestions for icebreakers

Here are some icebreakers you can use:

- *Question time*: Members of the group have to go round and chat with other people to find out which of these questions is applicable to them. Only one name is allowed against each question. Try to find a member of the group who can answer a question positively (only one name allowed against each question).
  - Who is a Scorpio?
  - Who can ride a horse?

- Who has two cats?
- Who can make a good curry?
- Who has been up the Eiffel tower?
- Who has bought a CD recently?
- Who regularly watches *EastEnders*?
- Who has concerns/worries about participating in this customer care programme?
- Who has a hobby that involves collecting things?
- Who supports a local football team?
- Who drives a red car?
- Who belongs to a club or society?

■ *What sort of car would you be and why*? Pose the question to the group, give them a minute or so to think about it, and then perhaps take the lead by answering the question yourself. Then go around the group asking each individual to answer.

■ *Impromptu discussion*: Give each member of the group a list of topics and give them a minute to choose one they would like to talk about briefly. Again, you may want to lead by speaking first. In this manner, you will be able to display roughly how long the speech should last. Topics might include:

- my first memory;
- my first day at school;
- my first best friend;
- a frock/outfit I remember;
- a holiday;
- a nickname;
- a pet;
- a play/film I saw;
- a prize I won;
- an object I'd save from a fire;
- home;
- time away from home etc.

Although the topic is given to one person, encourage other participants to chip in. Do take care with time management, however, and be prepared to step in and gently close the discussion, otherwise the session may turn into a prolonged version of 'all our yesterdays'.

- *Word association*: Give each person a word and ask them what it reminds them of. Use words related to the topics in the above icebreaker, such as 'holidays', 'friendship' or 'schooldays'.

- *Information exchange*: Split into pairs/threes to find out something of interest about the other person (why they came, special interests, holidays etc.) so that everyone knows at least one person reasonably quickly.

- *Alphabet soup*: The aim here is for participants to rearrange themselves into the alphabetical order of their forenames by sitting in the appropriate seat. This gives both the trainer and the participants the opportunity to remember names.

- *Bingo*: Ask group members to draw a grid of three-by-three squares, like a noughts and crosses grid. In each section they should insert a number of personal significance, from one to 50, for example, day, month or year of birth, anniversary date, age, child's age, shoe size, etc. Once everyone has filled in the grid, go round the group and ask each member to read out and mark off one of their numbers; in turn, any participant with the same number can also mark it off. Then exchange reasons why that number is significant. The first person to get a horizontal, vertical or diagonal line of three numbers should cry 'bingo'. Be prepared for the winner to ask for a prize!

A note on energisers

In sessions where participants have to take in a lot of information, some facilitators like to introduce energisers halfway through to help refresh participants. This is purely a matter of personal preference on the part of the facilitator.

Many of the icebreakers suggested above can be used as energisers if you have not employed them at the start of your session.

Two further possible energisers are given below, but note that they may be unsuitable for participants with disabilities:

- *Time to stretch*: All participants should stand up. One participant is asked to do an exercise or stretch. All other participants should then try to copy them. Choose a few people to take the lead with a different exercise for everyone to do. Warn participants to do only what is within their own comfort zone. Exercises could include shoulder shrugging; turning head slowly from left to right and stretching back gently at the same time; a full body stretch reaching towards the ceiling; or stretching out your arms and moving your fingers up and down. All these are stress relievers (see Chapter 8).

- *The birthday game:* Split the participants into two teams. Teams must arrange themselves in chronological order of their birthdays. This should be done as a race between teams.

Books of party games often have ideas that can be adapted as icebreakers or energisers. Do, however, bear in mind your anticipated group membership, and the previous advice regarding special needs, cultural differences etc.

Aim 2: Expressing concerns and creating a climate for learning

After the introduction and an icebreaker, it may be useful to canvass group feelings about undertaking the course. This can be done by getting people to talk to the person next to them about these feelings, or even, in the case of a small group, for the group to discuss the issue informally. This approach tends to anonymise the expression of specifically individual concerns and motives, and hence encourages a frank exchange of opinions and expectations.

Before starting the session in detail, a firm foundation for further progress can be made by drawing up an informal 'contract' between participants. A suggested format is given below. Avoid simply imposing this on participants. If you want people to genuinely 'buy in' to the proposed approach, it is far better to elicit and to suggest.

Aim 3: Understanding the aims of the course

Give the participants a handout detailing what they should be able to do on completion of the programme. For example, participants should be able to:

- identify the ingredients of excellent service and what it means in practice;

- identify more clearly who the customers are and what needs they have;

- have a better understanding of how to meet the special needs of customers from ethnic minority and other equal opportunity groups;

- deal more clearly and confidently with enquiries face to face and over the telephone;
- communicate and listen more effectively;
- compare strategies for handling both difficult customers and stressful situations;
- deal politely and assertively with customers who infringe library regulations;
- develop better working relationships and teambuilding within information services;
- suggest improvements to the department's services, and prepare a personal action plan.

Aim 4: Establishing the ground rules

After these concerns have been expressed, mention should be made of ground rules. Facilitators might want to start with a simple contract, such as the following ground rules for communication, where participants agree to:

- make simple, personal statements rather than talking about things in vague generalisations;
- avoid saying 'I can't' when I really mean 'I won't';
- pay attention to what I am really seeing, hearing and feeling, rather than imagining what someone else is thinking;
- avoid asking rhetorical questions, pretending I am asking for information, when what I really want to do is to make a statement;
- be specific, clear and direct in what I say, and not go on talking with lots of stories and examples;
- avoid saying 'you', 'we', 'one', 'it', 'they', 'the department' when I mean 'I';
- talk directly to the person I want to reach, rather than 'broadcasting' into the air or at the floor;
- avoid talking about the past when the issue is in the present;
- say where I stand on an issue;
- listen to others without making instant judgments;
- keep information confidential when I have agreed to do this.

Facilitators may prefer to use a flipchart and get group members to come up with their own list, based on any concerns raised by the group. For example, many people hate doing role plays, so a common concern is whether the course will contain any role play. Facilitators can then reassure group members that role plays do not feature in this particular programme.

Additional ground rules can also be added to the flipchart. These would be any additional rules to which the group agrees, for example, that mobile phones should be switched off or on silent mode.

Aim 5: Clarifying the role of the facilitator

Having established the ground rules, this leads nicely on to discussing the role of the facilitator. The material below could be used as a handout, although facilitators may prefer to write this out beforehand on a flipchart, or to scan the text and project it via PC onto a screen or whiteboard. Much depends on the venue and on the facilities available.

Remember: *facilis* is Latin for 'easy'. This means that facilitating is 'making easy'. A facilitator is therefore someone who makes learning easy. They are not expected to be a content expert – the content is derived from this training manual.

The facilitator's role is to guide and encourage participants through their learning experience in the following ways:

- enabling people to learn in a group, through the active involvement of the whole person in the process in order to develop knowledge, skills and positive attitudes;
- enabling people to take responsibility for their own learning and to control the way they work together as a learning group;
- providing learning opportunities, resources, encouragement and support for people to achieve their objectives and to meet their individual and group needs;
- empowering people to believe in themselves, to realise their own potential, and to overcome obstacles to their development;
- encouraging people to learn and to change in ways that make sense and feel right to them, as well as fitting in with their own values.

What is customer service?

Treat every customer as if they sign your pay-cheque – because they do. (Anon)

There are no traffic jams along the extra mile. (Roger Staubach)

Aims

The aims of this chapter are as follows:

- to identify the ingredients of good/bad/excellent service in practice;
- to recognise the importance of customers' expectations and feelings.

To assist with planning, Table 3.1 presents a suggested session plan.

Background

On a daily basis, we need the help and support of other people. Every contact that we make with others has elements of give and take, whether in a library, shop, restaurant, garage or wherever.

When we get the response that we want, we feel good about that contact. We have experienced a positive interaction which makes us want to repeat the experience.

Sometimes, we may feel that our daily contact with our customers, for example, students, members of the public, is just part of our daily routine, and is therefore somewhat humdrum and boring. On occasion, we all feel as if a robot could perform elements of our job. For customers, however, contact with us may not be routine. They have customer expectations and needs built into their feelings.

Table 3.1 Session plan – what is customer service?

Session	Aims	Content	Methods	Aids	Time (mins)
What is customer service?	To identify the constituents of good/bad/ excellent service in practice		T		5
		My customer service experiences	A	H/O	10
				F/C	10
	To recognise the importance of customers' expectations and feelings		T		5
Approx. total time (mins)					30

*A, activity (participants); F/C, flipchart; H/O, handout; P/I, Post-it notes; T, talk (facilitator)

In a busy working life, it is all too easy for customers to be faces in a crowd rather than individuals. However, they want to be treated as individuals, and as such, not merely processed as if they were a number. Consider encounters you have had yourself when you have been on the receiving end of customer service.

There have most likely been occasions when you have gone to buy something in a shop and then walked out because you could not get assistance or because the assistants seemed more interested in talking to their colleagues than in serving you. Perhaps you went to a restaurant where the service was so slow and the serving staff so sullen that, despite the good food on offer, you decided to go elsewhere in future. How often do you order goods and services on the internet simply to avoid encountering impersonal staff in customer service situations? It is quite common to try to avoid places and people with whom you have had a negative experience, and to seek out those who make you feel good about yourself.

This chapter relates to the session entitled 'What is customer service', and the associated activity involves participants identifying examples of good and bad service, and the facilitators capturing these examples on a flipchart. You can have two teams if you like, one giving examples of 'good' service and the other giving examples of 'bad' service. Alternatively, get participants to chat to the person next to them about one good and one bad experience. When they share with the group, don't just look superficially at the experience – analyse its different elements to understand what made it good or bad. In this way, you can relate it more closely to the participants' work situation.

For example a participant may describe a 'good' experience by saying that, when they were looking for a product in the supermarket, they asked a member of staff who actually stopped what they were doing and took them to the appropriate shelf, as opposed to just pointing towards another area of the store or directing them to another member of staff – the well known and frustrating 'bounce' technique. You can highlight the personalised nature of this positive attention, and how it makes the customer feel both special and valued.

Or, to give another example, a participant may describe a 'bad' experience by recounting a time when they phoned a company about a service and were passed on from one person to another – the 'bounce' again. In discussing this, it should be emphasised how poor service like this makes the customer feel unimportant and undervalued. There are case studies of both good and bad experiences at the end of this chapter. Use them as you will. You might wish to present participants with the account of the experience and get them to analyse it and then compare their analyses with the one provided. You might prefer to give participants the whole case studies and analyses to read or take away from the session or you may just wish to read and inwardly digest them yourself.

As an alternative to the activities on the session plan, there is a mini-questionnaire about what constitutes customer service. The chapter also includes the results of a survey on bad service. You may want to photocopy this as a handout for discussion, or scan it and show it on a screen or whiteboard via a PC. Choose the method that suits you best, and with which you are most comfortable.

When we come away from an interaction with a customer feeling good about helping them, we feel good about ourselves. We are not just another member of staff but somebody to be remembered. It is a win-win situation. This is something we visit later when we discuss life positions and the OK Corral (Chapter 9).

CHERISH your customers. This mnemonic may help you identify what customers want:

- Consideration
- *Help*

- *Expectations met*
- *Respect*
- *Individualisation* (to be treated as special, not just one of an amorphous mass of customers)
- *Support*
- *Honesty*

The key to so much of this is positive communication (Chapter 5), and later in this manual there are chapters devoted to this important topic, including questioning and listening skills (Chapter 6). Positive communication put into action can make both the communicator and the recipient feel good about each other. It does not have to be in the form of effusive praise, it can be as simple as a smile or a 'thank you'.

Dealing with other people, whether customers, colleagues or others, is an important part of our lives. How we provide help and support to others will influence their feelings. Later in this manual we discuss influencing styles (Chapter 9) and how they can impact on others. If you are stressed or depressed, your negative attitude can transmit itself to customers and can therefore have a negative impact on the service you are providing. You need to feel good about yourself and to recognise that the customers themselves are rarely the cause of your problems. Don't take it out on them. Dealing successfully with other people necessitates dealing successfully with yourself. This manual includes information and activities on issues such as confidence and assertiveness (Chapter 9) in order to help achieve this.

It is OK to be self-congratulatory. When you know you're doing your job well, give yourself a pat on the back. This is especially useful when no one else does so. Reflect on and enjoy your own achievements. Self-praise is a foundation that helps to counteract the negative experiences you may encounter on the way. It is OK, indeed, positively motivating to feel good about yourself. Later in the manual there is a session on what are we good at (Chapter 12) which both encourages and allows participants to do just that – to have positive feelings about themselves. In order to be respected by others, you first have to respect yourself.

As part of this session, we suggest that you explain to the participants how 'good' service exceeds customer expectations and 'bad' service fails to meet those expectations. We recognise that you can't always exceed customer expectations, especially as some customers have very high, if not unrealistic, expectations. However, we should at least try to live up to our own 'best practice' service expectations in order to benefit everyone.

Aim 1: Identifying the constituents of good/bad/excellent service in practice

My customer service experiences

In this activity, participants are required to list two or three businesses (shops, restaurants, garages, libraries, council offices, even departments within their own organisation) that they try to avoid dealing with because of unfair treatment or a poor service encounter in the past. On a sheet of paper, they should note the businesses in the first column and itemise the reasons they avoid them in the second column.

Next, the participants are asked to think of an occasion when they received good customer service, noting the business concerned along with itemised reasons as to why their experience was memorable or exceptional.

Participants can then briefly discuss their experiences with the participant sitting next to them before sharing the experiences with the group and the facilitator(s), who should concentrate on the reasons why the service experiences were good or bad. These can be written on a flipchart under the headings 'Good' and 'Bad'.

You may wish to refer to some of the case studies in this book for examples.

The Urban Life study on bad customer service

In 2003, the Urban Life group conducted a study on bad customer service experiences. Asking the question, 'What type of bad customer service have you experienced in the past four weeks?', the results were as follows:

- being put on hold during a phone call: 84 per cent;
- someone not returning your call: 63 per cent;
- being served by a cashier who was ignoring you: 60 per cent;
- asking shop staff a simple question to which they did not know the answer: 49 per cent;
- unable to find a member of staff in a supermarket: 40 per cent;
- having a problem with a product where the store did not apologise: 39 per cent;
- queuing to buy a train ticket for more than ten minutes: 26 per cent;
- none of the above: 3 per cent

Aim 2: Recognising the importance of customers' expectations and feelings

In any customer-focused service, one must define the customer's view of quality and then deliver to that level. Simply put, quality is what the customer says it is.

As we have said previously, some of your customers' expectations may well be beyond your power to deliver. Don't have sleepless nights over this. Nonetheless, think about what service quality means to your customers. Ideally, they will expect it to be:

- *Personal*
- *Efficient*
- *Responsive* (getting back to the customer quickly)
- *Fair*
- *Equitable* (even-handed)
- *Competent*
- *Timely*

and

- *Three-sixty degree* (all round and mutual)
- *Open* (both in the sense of being sincere and in terms of accessibility)
- *Polite* (courteous)
- *Informed* (about the customers and their needs)
- *Communicative* (keeping customers in the loop)
- *Authentic* (credible, believable)
- *Loyal* (to customers, in that it does what it says, is reliable, dependable and trustworthy)

In other words, service quality is PERFECT and TOPICAL – just the thing and just in time. It may be worth sharing this mnemonic with participants, perhaps via a flipchart.

Of course, this is a long laundry list – hence the word *ideally*. The key point to take away is the need to understand your customers' expectations and to consider how you can be proactive in meeting those expectations. To help with this, see Chapter 12 on action planning.

If you can treat customers as people, not just as a transaction or even an inconvenience, and give them your full attention (asking yourself

'What makes this person special?' can sometimes help here), then you contribute to your own feeling of self-worth and to the overall effectiveness of your organisation.

It is important to remember that colleagues are customers too, and the way that we respond to others at work is also relevant to service quality. Failure to perform our jobs can have a ripple effect, resulting in unhappy colleagues. This is covered further in Chapter 4.

As a bit of light relief, you might want to share the following quotations with participants:

> Welcome to customer services. We would like you to know your call is important to us, so we are going to leave you on hold for the next 20 minutes.

> Pre-recorded messages might as well say 'Press 1 for a long irrelevant list, press 2 to be kept on hold for 10 minutes, press 3 to be cut off'.

We have all been there!

Case studies of good and bad customer service

Throughout this book we provide illustrative, true-life examples of both good and bad customer service. Where the 'good' examples are concerned we have obtained the permission of those involved to identify them by name and company in our text. As for the 'bad' examples, you will appreciate that for legal reasons, the identities of those concerned have been withheld in order to protect the guilty (and the authors) from possible litigation...

Good customer service

We visited the Leaplish Park Leisure Centre in Kielder Forest, run by Northumbrian Water, and in the late afternoon were sitting on the patio outside The Boat Inn, considering returning later for an evening meal.

An employee of The Boat Inn (Mr Colin Hair) was collecting empty glasses and a menu from adjacent tables. As he passed, we asked to see the menu he was carrying. Mr Hair offered the menu, but advised that it was only valid until 5.30 pm, when it would be replaced by the evening menu (the time was 4.15 pm). We explained that we were considering returning for dinner, at which point he went into the restaurant and returned with two menus – one for each of us. He then advised us that as it was a busy weekend, it would be a good idea to book ahead. We explained that we usually dined early, and he suggested that 6.30 pm would be relatively quiet. We confirmed the booking and he offered to accompany us into the restaurant in order to select a table. While there, he pointed out that as one large table was reserved for a hen party arriving at 7.00 pm, we might wish to select a table away from that area. (As it turned out, the party included both teenagers and grandmas, and was perfectly well-behaved.) As we left, he thanked us for our booking, and said that he looked forward to seeing us return later.

Analysis

Our immediate requirement was to see a menu. Had Mr Hair simply handed us the afternoon menu, in basic terms, our customer needs would have been met. However, he took an immediate interest in further defining our customer requirement, and in tailoring his response to our needs. At every stage, he aimed to exceed our expectations, and took a personal interest in maximising our potential enjoyment of both the facilities and the services provided by The Boat Inn. In doing so, he acknowledged us as individuals, with individual needs, and made us feel that we were highly valued customers. The whole experience made us feel very positive about the evening ahead. (As an aside, the meal was also excellent – but even had it not been, we could certainly have had no complaints about the service we received.) The immediate benefit to the company concerned was that they received an unsolicited, personal testimonial from us, which you are now reading. This is the best sort of advertising that you can get – and it comes free. They are also likely to see repeat business from us, and some of you may even be tempted to call in if you are in the area. All this because one of their employees went out of his way to provide the best customer service that he could deliver.

Footnote

At the end of all this, we sought out Mr Hair, congratulated him on his excellent customer service skills, and obtained his agreement to include him in our book. We also completed a customer satisfaction survey to pass on to his manager. His obvious delight in this feedback serves as a useful reminder to us all that when you do receive good customer service, even from colleagues, it is positively reinforcing for all concerned when you personally acknowledge it. While it is certainly OK to feel good about yourself, it is even more beneficial and confidence-building when someone else feels good about you, and tells you so.

Bad customer service

We bought a new motor home from a major national supplier with a main branch in the local area. The actual sale was carried out very efficiently, and the salesperson was charming, personable and extremely helpful. Once the actual sale was completed, we were handed over to the company's customer support or 'after-sales' service. Nevertheless, on subsequent visits to the main branch, the salesperson always remembered our names, and made a point of conversing with us.

The after-sales service was responsible for servicing, for the supply of spares, and for running the onsite motor home and caravan storage area – which was extensive. When the van was delivered it was minus the fitted carpets in the habitation area. The company advised us that it had ordered a set from the manufacturer, and that delivery would take place within two weeks. Three weeks later, the carpets had still not arrived. Finally, our friendly salesperson (who was not part of the after-sales team) took it upon himself to chase up the items, and telephoned us to tell us that the carpets had arrived, were in the main store, and that he had asked the servicing department (who still had the spare keys to the motor home) to install them. When we telephoned the company after-sales team, they advised us that the carpets were 'in the van'. We assumed (wrongly) that this meant that they had been unpacked and fitted. We visited the storage area on the next Friday, fully intending to take the vehicle out that weekend. When we arrived, the carpets were indeed in the motor home, but were still sealed in plastic wrapping. When we unwrapped them and tried to fit them ourselves, it was immediately obvious that they were the wrong items, for a different model of motor home. Replacement items were ordered, and took a further two weeks to arrive. Once again, the still-packed items were simply dumped in the motor home. Fortunately, when we unpacked them ourselves for a second time, they fitted.

Some time later, a friend advised us to fit an additional security lock on the main habitation area access door, as the standard locking mechanism was quite flimsy compared with the main vehicle doors. The company agreed to fit a proprietary security lock for us. Once again, they gave us a completion date that slipped by several days, with no convincing explanation as to why. On top of this, when we collected the new keys, we found they didn't work. Although we suspected that the new lock had simply been fitted incorrectly, the company attributed the problem to a 'manufacturing fault', and said that they would have to source a replacement part from the manufacturer. This would entail a further two-week delay, as the manufacturer was based in Italy. It was therefore a 'pleasant surprise' that the fault was rectified within 24 hours.

As motor home storage sites are at a premium, we considered ourselves fortunate to obtain a pitch at this main branch in our local area. This would be convenient not only for our own ease of access, but also for servicing purposes. Such storage does not come cheap, but has the advantage of a 'highly secure' storage area, with '24-hour patrols' and 'full CCTV coverage'. Some four months after we started to use the 'secure storage', the company phoned to inform us that there had been a break-in, and that the catalytic converter (worth some £1,100) had been stolen from our vehicle. On immediately visiting the site, we were advised that approximately 30 such converters had been stolen from their new stock, and approximately 20 from other motor homes in the storage area. We were shown a large gap that had been cut in the security fence, where the razor wire had also been removed. Despite being so obvious, the closest estimate that the company could give as to when the break-in took place, was 'some time between Saturday and Tuesday night'. We immediately entered into correspondence with the company, and advised them that we considered them fully liable for replacement of the item, as our storage contract was with them, and not with their subcontracted security company. Almost one year and several formal letters later, although we have had verbal assurances from the company that this is 'going through the courts', we have had no written acknowledgment of our claim. At time of writing, we are preparing to take them to small claims court.

Analysis

This sad saga started so promisingly, with an efficient, helpful sales person carefully shepherding us through every stage of the sale, up to the point of delivery. However, in true apocryphal style, once we had 'paid up front', everything changed for the worse. Shoddy after-sales service and poor quality-assurance meant that not only were the wrong carpets ordered in the first place, but delivery forecasts were neither met nor updated, and even when the order eventually arrived – prompted by the intervention of a non-specialist member of staff – it was neither checked nor fitted, thus missing the fact that it was the wrong item. Even when the replacement order arrived, this was not unpacked to double-check that at least this time, the correct item had been obtained. This demonstrates little or no interest in customer satisfaction, and shows an inability, or perhaps even a disinterest to learn from the most basic mistakes. Continuous improvement of the service provided? Not in this firm. No chance.

The pattern is repeated with the faulty security lock. No check on the quality or even the basic functionality of the fitted item, and a transparent attempt to lay the blame on 'faulty materials' from the supplier, when clearly it had been fitted incorrectly by maintenance staff.

As for the theft of the catalytic converter, this company has so little interest in satisfying its customers that it does not even bother to reply to their letters. The overall impression is of an organisation that thinks the world owes it a living, and that appears to run itself for the benefit of its own employees, rather than for its unfortunate customers. They are one of the few providers of 'secure' motor home and caravan storage in the local area, and appear to think that this gives them an excuse not to try too hard. Indeed, the company appears so disinterested in maintaining high standards across the board, that it even seems incapable of properly monitoring the internal security task that it has subcontracted to a local firm. As a result, the company is now being taken to court. In direct contrast to the previous case study, this is a case of the worst possible sort of advertising, which is anything but free.

Footnote

We feel sorry for the salesperson, who appeared genuinely committed to providing a quality service, to the extent that he even intervened outside of his immediate departmental area in an attempt to overcome the inadequacies of his colleagues in another department. We got the impression that this was not the first time. Well-motivated, customer-oriented people do not tend to join organisations where the corporate ethos is both inward-looking and self-serving. Of those that do so, the best are usually the very first to leave. That sales person has indeed now left the company.

Social networking undoes the international superstore

A customer checked the website of a major, international company, which provides a complete home furnishing concept throughout Europe, to see if an item of furniture she had ordered was yet in stock. As the website indicated 'nil stock', the customer then telephoned the company for a progress report, and was advised to call back in a week's time, by which time the shipment should have arrived from the overseas supplier.

The customer then moved on to a social networking site, and quite by chance, noticed a feed that included a photo of the superstore in question, and some comment by someone who clearly lived in the vicinity. Taking a chance on benefiting from the milk of human kindness, the customer then quite brazenly asked the local networker if they would be able to do a physical stock check for them. Surprisingly, the kind networker agreed to this request, and less than 45 minutes later responded on the social network, not only confirming that the item was in fact in stock, but also including a photograph of it.

Sadly, the customer indicated that this was not the first time that this had happened, which was why she had felt moved to ask for an independent, physical stock check in the first place. The customer then visited the store and obtained the item she had ordered. What she said to the company, or what their response was, is unfortunately not recorded.

Lessons learned

- Make sure that your stock recording systems are robust, and that you have built-in checks and measures to maintain their accuracy.

- Don't rely absolutely on computer-based stock recording systems – particularly where libraries are concerned. Such systems should certainly be at the heart of your stock control, but it is worth enhancing the process with a programme of physical spot checks or stock sampling to highlight 'lost' or misplaced items that are beyond the horizon of your computer's visibility, and would remain lost in the system without direct human intervention – i.e. through use of the good-old Mark 1 Eyeball. Such spot-check or stock-sampling activity should not be seen as something to consider during those rare 'slack periods' when your shelvers have time on their hands. Recognise their importance by programming them in as part of your routine.

- Work hard to establish an environment in which your employees take a keen, personal interest in efficient customer service. Avoid the 'computer says no' approach at all costs. The computer is a tool – no more and no less – and the customer is in contact with *you*, not a system.

4

Who are our customers?
The customer service chain

- Because the customer has a NEED, we have a job to do.
- Because the customer has a choice, we must be the BETTER CHOICE.
- Because the customer has sensibilities, we must be CONSIDERATE.
- Because the customer has an urgency, we must be QUICK.
- Because the customer is unique, we must be FLEXIBLE.
- Because the customer has high expectations, we must EXCEL.
- Because the customer has INFLUENCE, we have the hope of MORE customers.
- BECAUSE of the customer WE exist.

(Sears Department Store Coffee Shop, Union Square, San Francisco)

We need to understand, and understand deeply, the role of the library in our end-users' lives, work, research, and play... (Stephen Abram)

Library organizations, like so many other types of organizations today, face the need for significant transformation ... in how they meet the challenges of staying relevant and meeting the needs and expectations of their various constituent groups. (Maureen Sullivan)

Users will choose the library only if their library experience integrates well with their own view of themselves and their priorities... (Joan Frye Williams)

Aims

The aims of this chapter are as follows:

- to identify more clearly the different kinds of customer;
- to recognise the special needs of different customers;
- to recognise from whom we receive service in general;
- to recognise our internal customers.

To assist with planning, Table 4.1 presents a suggested session plan.

Background

In this chapter and training session, we are obtaining more detailed information about our customers in order to identify their needs more

Table 4.1	Session plan – who are our customers? The customer service chain

Session	Aims	Content	Methods	Aids	Time (mins)
Who are our customers	To identify more clearly the different kinds of customers		T	F/C	10
	To recognise the special needs of different customers	Who we are and what we need	A		10
		Customer rainbow	A	H/O	20
Customer service chain	To recognise from whom we receive service in general		T		
	To recognise who our internal customers are	Service to and from	A	H/O	10
Approx. total time (mins)					50

*A, activity (participants); F/C, flipchart; H/O, handout; P/I, Post-it notes; T, talk (facilitator)

accurately. This is not only helpful in terms of developing better working relationships but also encourages teambuilding.

In our daily lives, we both give and receive service. The customers to whom we give service are the people who keep us in gainful employment. Whatever task we are performing, everything we do affects the satisfaction – or dissatisfaction – of our customers.

Ask yourself:

- What do your customers expect of you?
- What do you expect of your customers?

Satisfying customers' requirements must be our main aim. We can do this only by putting quality into everything we do. To achieve our objective, we must be seen as an organisation that:

- knows our customers' requirements;
- provides services based on these requirements;
- consistently meets these requirements.

Our customer community is not simply a broad, amorphous public. Every community can be broken down into subgroups, each with its own needs. Professional associations have recognised this and produced guidelines accordingly. Examples include: *Guidelines for University Library Services to Undergraduate Students* (American Library Association, 2005); *Guidelines for Library Service to Babies and Toddlers* (IFLA, 2006); *Guidelines on Library and Information Services for Older Adults* (Canadian Library Association, 2002) and *Guidelines on Library and Information Services for People with Disabilities* (Canadian Library Association, 1997).

If we can identify characteristics that identify different public groupings, we can plan accordingly to meet actual and potential needs. In the case of the latter, services may be available (or could be made available) that the customer does not know about. We have to create an environment in which such needs may be expressed and identified. This involves being able to understand customers' needs and behaviours in order to categorise them more effectively, to offer them the right service at the right time, but above all, to persuade them that the service they are offered is adapted to their needs and is the ideal solution.

A simple mnemonic which can help us to develop an approach which first identifies and then responds effectively to the needs of our customer base is 'SURE':

- *Strategic planning*
- *Understanding*
- *Response management*
- *Execution excellence*

There are many different kinds of customer. You might recognise some of the following:

- *The hacker*: The hacker is knowledgeable about ICTs, and attaches great importance to the technical aspects of the service on offer. They will willingly test the system to its limits and will be delighted if they manage to 'crack' elements of it. But do they tell you?

- *The hanger-on*: The hanger-on does not understand the service so trusts the staff to be able to deliver. This is all very well if they are new to the service, but some users can play on this, never using their own initiative, preferring to rely constantly on staff for support. On their next visit they may approach a different member of staff to help with the same sort of service requirement.

- *The happy*: The happy customer will cheerfully focus on common interests with the service provider, provided the staff member knows how to establish a good interpersonal relationship. Being friendly to customers is good, but being overly friendly with them may not be the ideal approach, and does have its own risks. If they feel they have a good relationship with a particular staff member, such customers may seek them out during their every visit. There is also the danger that this type of relationship may escalate into unwanted attention.

- *The haggler*: Hagglers fancy themselves as negotiators who get the best out of the service, sometimes bypassing certain staff and homing in on more senior staff. Like the hacker, they try to test the system to its limits, but in this case they are trying to 'crack' the staff. They can be difficult customers.

- *The hitchhiker*: The hitchhiker is free-riding on the back of your service. Examples include the student who uses the university library as a social club; the tramp who uses the public library to shelter from the rain; the homeless or even just plain lonely person who lingers over one cup of coffee in a snack bar over lunch-hour. They may not actually 'use' the core services, but certainly affect how other customers do.

- *The hopeful*: Such neophytes are attentive to the service provider whom they respect as knowledgeable. They hope to develop into active and informed service users. Unlike the hangers-on, the hopeful are prepared to learn to be independent service users and can develop into the type of customer we all enjoy serving.

Consider the library customer manifesto below:

- I would like to deal with an ethical service provider.
- I would like to know how your services operate.
- I would like to avail myself of your services according to my timetable, not yours, whether it be at midday, midnight, Sunday or on New Year's Eve.
- I would like to know when something is wrong with your service and how you are going to address this.
- I would like to tell you when you are getting things wrong – and when you are getting them right.
- I would like to connect with other users who share my interests.
- I would like to have some input into your service development.
- I would like to help shape services that I would personally find useful.
- I would like to know what is on the horizon for the service and the direction it will take.

Most of these needs go well beyond the basics, and relate to wanting to be in a partnership with the service provider. Most of these needs are also geared to the 'physical world'. Given that many services are now operating online, can you consider more 'needs' that take account of virtual environments, such as IT-based remotely managed learning media like Blackboard™, which is widely used in UK universities?

Customer needs and the concomitant expectations are often set by other organisations, for example, banks, airlines, fast-food outlets etc. So, in a sense, we are competing with organisations dissimilar to our own. In the past, many of these organisations based their services on customer segmentation, where the more the customer was prepared to pay, the better the service they received. By 'segmentation', we are referring to the process of allocating customers to a particular group that shares some perceived customer needs. However, customer service based on such segmentation usually follows an oversimplified philosophy, and is often far too 'broad-brushed' in its approach. Intuitively, this approach often seems reasonable, and in some cases, successful, particularly where service industries are concerned. Yet this approach can also result in lost customers and missed opportunities, especially as companies strive to differentiate themselves through the delivery of more personalised customer service. A better philosophy to follow is: 'for every customer, the appropriate service' (Van Everen, 2002).

Another concept you may encounter in the literature is that of customer relationship management (CRM), through which an attempt is made to anticipate and satisfy the needs and demands of customers. CRM brings together a number of customer-related ideas to try to provide a holistic approach to meeting the customer's needs and managing the customer lifecycle.

Just because our customers may have no alternative to using our service, it does not mean we can be complacent about this. As the above manifesto indicates, customers want to give feedback and this can adversely affect the institutional reputation. Even 'adequate' service is likely to be registered as 'poor' by customers when compared with other institutions. Most dissatisfied customers won't tell you about their dissatisfaction, but they are likely to tell friends and colleagues. In this way, what started as a mild degree of dissatisfaction may even end up exaggerated into a horror story.

Consider how your customers' needs are changing and how their expectations may also change so that they appear to be more demanding. For example, given rising education costs, students may expect more value for money from their teaching and support staff. Academic staff may feel pressurised to produce more output, often with fewer resources.

Your standards of customer service are likely to need to be on a permanent upward curve. You need to consider how effective your customer service is and how it might be improved (see Chapter 10). Finally, if you can't exceed expectations, you can at least manage them.

Aim 1: To identify more clearly the different kinds of customer

Consultation at Huddersfield University

Huddersfield University has produced a customer charter based on:

- consultation with library staff focus groups, using the internet to research best practice in customer service standards;
- canvassing both staff and students for input via questionnaires and informal focus groups;
- asking all 'customer-facing' library and computing staff for feedback on the comments made by both staff and students.

The university also makes use of customer comment cards, recording comments, complaints and compliments in a dedicated a database. The library management group then discusses any issues twice yearly, and a synopsis of feedback is put online for general access.

The library also documents the different forms of consultation with both internal and external users, focusing on obtaining 'best fit' related to customer segmentation, and aiming to use the most appropriate form of consultation for each segment (see Figure 4.1).

The customer segments are as follows:

- undergraduates and taught postgraduates;
- support staff;
- international students;
- students with disabilities;
- collaborative provision users;
- academics and researchers;
- external customers.

In formalising and structuring its consultative approach, the university produced a strategy document in which the key elements were:

- an emphasis on the central importance of consulting with customers, of encouraging feedback, of taking appropriate action based on customer suggestions and of communicating outcomes back to the customers;
- maintaining a clear focus on the national context as regards consultation, for example the national student survey;
- making best use of the existing university framework, with focus groups for quality audits, and student consultation panels within individual schools;
- incorporating local context input, such as that generated within the university computing and library services departments.

The key to success in this comprehensive consultation process was to ensure that the customers' needs and expectations were clearly understood, and that services were then delivered accordingly. Having identified these needs, it was then important to instil and maintain a culture of excellent customer service at all levels of the organisation.

The university was also aware of the need not to overburden busy students with excessive consultation. Research shows that it is often extremely difficult to engage students in surveys or in focus groups. With

Figure 4.1 Customer segmentation at Huddersfield University

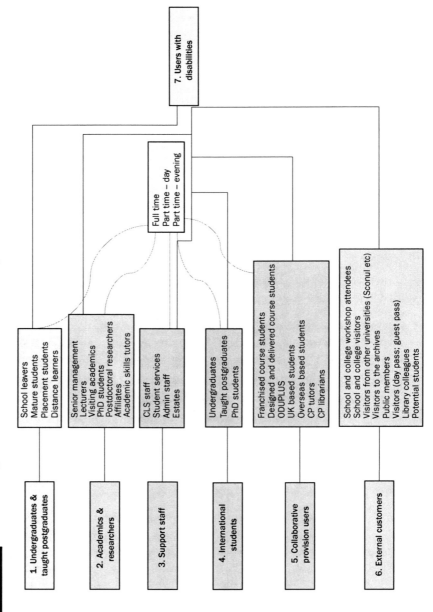

this in mind, the university keeps questionnaires to a minimum, and has developed a more focused approach to consultation on specific issues.

The approach can be summarised as follows:

- Questionnaires are used where consultation and feedback are required across a broad range of customer groups. These surveys are increasingly communicated via e-mail and administered online as the university community has universal access to computers. Occasionally, however, surveys are administered in paper format, for example for external customer groups.

- Focus groups are deployed for in-depth discussions about specific issues. Attendance at such focus groups is encouraged by offering financial incentives and refreshments.

- User groups and student panels are arranged throughout the academic year. Subject librarians participate in these on a regular basis to ask for views and to respond to questions. These panels can be effective for reaching customers who use the library rarely. By contrast, questionnaires and focus groups are more likely to attract active users of the service.

The customer charter is now displayed throughout the library, and is reproduced in the library handbook.

For further details on the consultation and feedback process, see: *http://www2.hud.ac.uk/cls/library/haveyoursay/*

Aim 2: To recognise the special needs of different customers

Who we are and what we need

In this activity, participants will identify and relate to many different types of customer. During this process, they will also identify a variety of perceived needs. Such needs can usually be categorised as follows:

- your organisation already meets this requirement;

- your organisation should offer this service, but currently does not;

- you may be capable of offering all or part of this service, but there are funding and resource implications;

- your organisation sees this requirement as a 'blue-sky' need, which realistically, you are unlikely to be able to meet in the foreseeable future.

We hope the exercise helps participants to exhibit facets of their customer care knowledge – not only of their internal and external customers, but also of the facilities and services that may or may not be on offer to cater for their needs.

In short, the task is for participants to:

- identify their customers;
- decide what their needs are.

Many needs will be specific to certain client groups; others will apply to most customers. Participants should write their decisions on a flipchart divided into two columns, with identified customers in one column and their specialist needs in the other. Once completed, the flipchart content can be shared with the group.

Table 4.2 presents some customer categorisation completed by actual groups of mixed library staff in a customer care training session, and exemplifies the approaches taken by group members, some of their ideas, and some humorous asides.

Table 4.2   **Example of customer categorisation completed by some library services staff**

Specific customer categories	Special needs/library services
Male/female	Different toilets, baby changing, child care facilities, Flexible opening hours, tailored to different lifestyles Refreshments
Our full-time/ part-time students	Access to resources, books, CD-ROMs etc Guidance/user education Accommodation Equipment, e.g. PCs, photocopiers, scanners, audiovisual media Technical support Welcoming environment Knowledgeable staff with a good attitude, patience and ICT skills Flexible opening hours Flexible loan periods Flexible borrowing rights Available subject staff Appropriate equipment Food & drink available No fines Non-robotic staff Miracles

| Table 4.2 | Example of customer categorisation completed by some library services staff (*Cont'd*) |

Specific customer categories	Special needs/library services
Freshers/ freshmen/ first-year students	All of the above plus More advice/direction because of limited experience
Mature students	All of the above plus [Re]introduction to services on offer Peace and quiet away from the family
Undergraduate/ postgraduate students from other universities	Reference-only facilities? Reciprocal arrangements?
Prospective students/ secondary school children	Reference-only facilities? Orientation sessions Prospectus and information about courses
Students with special needs	Ramps, auto doors Special equipment, e.g. Braille readers Adequate lifts Adequate toilets Trained staff, e.g. to use evacuation chairs in case of fire when lifts inoperable
Access/widening participation/ foundation year	[Re]introduction to services on offer Orientation sessions Basic guides
Distance/ franchise learners	Remote access Online help and support
Our academic staff/faculty	All of the above plus Availability of set texts Ordering of recommended books Library that is an extension of their office 'Queue jump' facility High expectations
Our non-academic/ support staff	Similar rights to academic staff? Administrative support, ordering resources etc, enquires about orders Equal commitment Friendly
Staff from other universities	Reference-only facilities Reciprocal arrangements

Table 4.2	Example of customer categorisation completed by some library services staff (Cont'd)

Specific customer categories	Special needs/library services
Retired staff from our university	Reference-only facilities Limited borrowing rights
Members of the public	Link with public library Remote access
Students on exchange programmes	Short-term service Liaison
International students and staff	PR – multilingual, cultural differences Signage in variety of languages* Staff with language skills Books/articles in their own language Newspapers from their own countries Translation service
Publishers, book sellers etc	PR

*In one academic library we visited, we noticed that the library signage was in English only, which was somewhat disappointing given how many international students attended the institution. Indeed, even the contractors had multilingual 'wet paint' signs, albeit doctored to include a Geordie 'translation' (Figure 4.2). For a non-vandalised version of this sign, see Nicholas Clark's photostream on Flickr: *http://www.flickr.com/photos/34063820@N00/206339056/* (accessed 16 November 2009).

Figure 4.2	Multilingual 'wet paint' sign, doctored to include a Geordie 'translation'

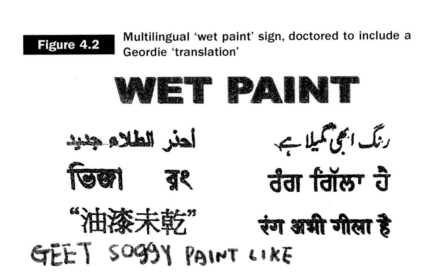

Exemplar: The watching wall – Christchurch Polytechnic Institute of Technology

Background

The watching wall was set up when the library was built in 1999. Built as a learning centre, incorporating library services, learning services, disability services, e-learning and a language self-access centre, the aim was to showcase both new technology and accessibility. With the number of international students growing every year, the watching wall provided access to worldwide broadcasting for international and language students. The 12 televisions connected to (at the time) the largest set of satellite receiving dishes in the south island of New Zealand, providing access to 25–30 channels. The School of Electro-technology used the project in its teaching of electrical engineering, and was responsible for the maintenance and development of the technology.

Feedback at the time of setup was very positive. International students would take headphones, select a channel, and make themselves comfortable on a beanbag. Language tutors encouraged their students to come in and watch the foreign language channels.

With the growth of the internet and the availability of news and foreign language newspapers via the web, the original benefits of the wall have been largely lost in recent years. Language students still use it, and many students do still enjoy it as a 'timeout'. But in no way does this diminish the forward-thinking, customer-focus of this initiative back when it was introduced in 1999.

The university is now looking at what it can replace the wall with. Some of the original television sets need to be replaced, and the university is looking into replacing them with a single large screen that can be used in different ways. The university subscribes to E-Cast (*http://www.e-cast.co.nz/home/education.html*), which provides live streaming of international and domestic television channels, and it is also looking at ways of using this to update both the hardware and technology used in the watching wall.

For more information on the watching wall, see: *http://library.cpit.ac.nz/*

Exemplar: Something fishy in the library – Murray State University

'The initial impetus for this initiative was actually an attempt to make a bad situation a little better.' The coffee shop in the library was not generating enough profit to satisfy the Director of Food Services, so he cut the number of hours it would be open. His original proposal called for it to be open during the afternoon for just a few hours. Because Murray State has a large population of 'heavy studiers' who come to the library in the late evening and spend several hours, a counter-proposal was made that the coffee shop would be open at night, and would offer meals. The coffee shop was not equipped at that time to offer full meals, but the solution of sushi was hit upon for several reasons. It is incredibly popular with many young Americans; Murray State has a large population of Asian students; and sushi does not require much processing or storage space. The sushi was originally purchased from a restaurant in the local town, and once students knew about it, the sushi sold out every evening. Eventually, negotiations resulted in the coffee shop being opened for a much longer period of time – from early in the morning until nearly midnight. Once this took place, more sushi was made available, and it still regularly sells out.

No pilot scheme was run, as such, and the first few weeks of the service saw only small amounts of sushi purchased from the local restaurant. Once it was noticed that it sold out very quickly, the amount purchased was increased. Now, the university makes its own sushi.

When the initiative was first announced in the library, it met with some incredulity from other administrators, but student response demonstrates its success: the speed with which the sushi sells out speaks for itself.

The university continues to monitor how much sushi it sells, so that it can adjust its rate of production to match. The library itself is currently involved in a number of negotiations with other campus units to increase the services offered in the building. An area of the library is being renovated in order to house the university copy and print services, giving students and faculty the ability to produce high-quality print jobs while in the building. This is already in the planning process. Beyond that, the library is also in talks about creating a writing centre for students.

The customer rainbow

This activity is more complex and wide-ranging than the previous, flipchart-based activity, and the first version of it requires some preparatory work on the facilitators' part, as explained below. While it is more complex, if you are going to run a number of customer care workshops, you may find it worth doing the preparation in order to build up some customer profiles for use in future activities.

Version one: creating fictional customers

The bands of the spectrum are used to represent various customer characteristics. For example:

- *red*: gender
- *orange*: ethnicity
- *yellow*: educational background
- *green*: subject/area of interest
- *blue*: level of interest
- *purple*: number of hours worked

Printed onto appropriately coloured strips, each band breaks into different elements. For example:

- *gender*
  - male
  - female
- *ethnicity*
  - White – British
  - White – Irish
  - White – European (EU)
  - White – European (non-EU)
  - White and Black Caribbean
  - White and Black African
  - White and Asian
  - Asian or Asian British
  - Black or Black British – Caribbean
  - Black or Black British – African
  - Chinese
- *educational background*
  - still at school
  - educated to O level or equivalent
  - educated to A level or equivalent
  - educated to degree level or equivalent
  - postgraduate or equivalent level

- *subject area of interest*
  - art and design
  - business
  - education
  - engineering/computer science
  - health/medicine
  - humanities
  - law/legal studies
  - music/performing arts
  - sciences
  - social sciences
- *level of interest*
  - beginner
  - intermediate
  - advanced/expert
- *number of hours worked*
  - 35 hours or more per week
  - 25 or more per week
  - 15 or more per week
  - 5 or more per week
  - do not work
- *employment status*
  - higher/intermediate managerial/admin/professional
  - supervisory/clerical/junior managerial/admin/professional
  - skilled manual workers
  - semi-skilled/unskilled manual workers
  - on benefit/unemployed

The different elements can be adjusted to suit your client group. For example, as regards ethnicity, one can use the UK census data divisions, as shown above. Alternatively one might simply use 'English is first language' and 'English is second language'. In terms of education level, a public library will have one client group that is still at school, while a university library can probably discount the first two categories.

Likewise, subject/area of interest is also institution-specific, and it is possible that employment categories would be more pertinent.

Cut out the colour-coded strips, keeping them in their particular colour band. You may need to tailor the strips to suit the particular client group; for example, if you know that the particular customer you are profiling is a child, you will need either to eliminate the violet band or say that this pertains to the child's parents/carers.

Participants divide into groups. Each group picks one strip of each colour, putting them all together to assemble their own customer profile. Some combinations may prove nonsensical, in which case, groups can either choose another strip of the appropriate colour, or omit that particular element from the profile they are constructing.

The participants' next task is to flesh out these bare bones of a profile to create a fictional customer biography.

Once the groups have finished, they swap their biography with another group, and then discuss the possible needs that the customer profiled in that particular biography may have with regards to the service they are offering.

Version two: rainbow consequences

An alternative way of using this activity is to play a game of 'consequences' using a sheet of A4 and the following headings:

- gender;
- ethnicity;
- educational background;
- subject area of interest;
- level of interest;
- number of hours worked/type of work done.

One participant fills in the first line as appropriate, folds down the page so that their contribution is no longer visible, and then passes it to the participant on their right. This process is then repeated around the group until each line has been completed. Each member of the group now has a basic profile and can use the space underneath it to make notes about the customer. Participants can then get into groups to decide on the needs of one or more of the customers profiled.

For this activity, you may want to write the element choices on a flipchart or whiteboard or distribute a handout containing the elements listed previously.

Case study: 'Give us a bash at the bangers and mash...'

The BBC2 series, *The Great British Menu*, featured 'the nation's finest chefs competing to honour the men and women from all three forces serving in Afghanistan with a glorious homecoming dinner that captures the authentic taste of home'.

In the Welsh heat, the suggested menus included the following

- *Starters*:
    - Welsh rarebit rabbit ('up-market' cheese on toast with rabbit meat and garnish)
    - poached chicken with pea ravioli and cheese 'foam'
- *Fish courses*:
    - sea bass with cockles, bacon and laver bread
    - smoked eel with pigs' trotters, creamed cauliflower, and maple and sherry vinegar
- *Main courses*:
    - lamb with umble pie (lambs tongue, heart, kidneys, liver)
    - loin of wild rabbit, asparagus and mushroom mousse and smoked butternut
- *Desserts*:
    - summer fruit pudding with honey and lavender cream
    - strawberries with jelly and ice cream

One of the present authors served in the armed forces for 25 years, taking part in numerous operations and exercises abroad. The standard of field catering has improved markedly since his early retirement in 1991, with 'semi-permanent' encampments such as Camp Bastion in Afghanistan now boasting well-known commercial fast-food outlets to supplement the official catering services. Indeed, the influence of the American contingent in such locations now means that the availability of such luxuries as New York strip steaks and Weber kettle barbecues from the Commissary store takes the 'fast-food' equation into an entirely different realm of existence. (This portrayal of the culinary delights available in Camp Bastion should in no way be taken as diminishing either the difficulty of the task or of the demanding conditions in which our troops are working in this particular theatre of operations.)

Nevertheless, for those based at or deployed to more remote forward operating bases, 'composite rations' or 'compo' is still very much the order of the day. These days, extensive use is made of dehydrated foods, and although these are highly nutritional and well-balanced in dietary terms – i.e. good 'soldier fuel' – few would argue that they could ever compete with 'home cooking'. Thus, as has always been the case, for today's soldier, sailor or airman (or airwoman), away from home and serving in some perhaps remote location, 'home thoughts from abroad' still feature favourite and fondly remembered dishes and food items that are not available locally.

Thus, while the artistry and culinary imagination of the menu proposed above are undoubtedly laudable, its worth as an exercise in keenly observed and researched customer service is highly questionable. Indeed, it is likely that the programme never seriously addressed the actual customer requirements of homecoming troops, and was more of a self-indulgent, media-focused exercise in which top chefs competed head-to-head, with the heats judged by non-military 'foodies' with little or no real feel for what our lads and lasses were yearning for as regards 'good grub'. I make no apologies for what may seem to be a rather harsh judgment here, as my loyalties are, and always will be clearly focused on the needs of the customer – in this particular case, arguably the most professional, dedicated armed forces in the world – a somewhat deserving bunch of customers indeed.

In establishing what food items the 'average' serviceman/woman looks forward to on their welcome return to Blighty, I have consulted past and present incumbents, ranging from those who, like myself, are of Falklands/first Gulf War vintage, to young men who are still serving and who anticipate further tours of duty in Afghanistan. Not surprisingly, such culinary delights as pea ravioli, cheese foam, sea bass and smoked butternut squash do not figure on their 'most wanted' lists. Regardless of generation, there is a beautiful simplicity in what many of them *really* yearn or yearned for:

- mum's Sunday dinner – roast beef with the full works;
- 'proper' battered cod, chips and mushy peas from the local chippy;
- a 'proper' butcher-made pork pie, and local pork sausages;
- a curry 'blow-out' in an Indian/Pakistani restaurant in their home town (army curries may be good, but they're no substitute);
- hearty 'stick to your ribs' puds (yes – even in subtropical climes), such as steamed syrup sponge, spotted dick etc.;
- good, strong, English cheeses and pickles;

- real ale (no change there then...)
- and, on a regional note, a young Geordie rifleman waxed lyrical about a saveloy dip with pease pudding, just going to show that it's all about 'individual' needs, not 'segmentation'.

The list above makes interesting reading when you compare it with the winning menu – which was judged not by the resident panel of 'foodies', but by the viewing public:

- *Starter*: salad of Aberdeen Angus beef, carrots, horseradish & Shetland black potatoes)
- *Fish course*: masala spiced monkfish with red lentils, and pickled carrots and coconut
- *Main course*: Lonk lamb Lancashire hotpot, pickled red cabbage, carrots and leeks
- *Dessert*: treacle tart with Jersey clotted cream and raspberry ripple coulis

So, good old roast beef with horseradish, curried fish, lancashire hotpot, and treacle tart – now that *is* the stuff to give the troops. Know your customer.

Case study: 'Boy Wonder'

A major European high-tech engineering company had a young, thrusting sales and marketing executive who had enjoyed great success in sales campaigns both in Western Europe and in North America. His advancement within the company had been meteoric, and on the crest of this wave of personal success he was selected to lead a sales team travelling to the Far East, to potentially win a multi-million pound export contract.

On arrival in the country, he headed up the presentation team and delivered his usual highly professional sales pitch. The series of presentations to government departments and to representatives of the local armed forces was programmed to take place over three days, with the usual lavish entertainment and formal dinners for the potential customer, all funded by the company. By day three, he realised that he was not communicating well with his potential customer, and had failed to establish that 'special relationship' which his personal charisma and technical efficiency had always established in the past. Instead of his company winning the contract, it was awarded to a European competitor.

Following this failure, the company carried out detailed research to establish what had gone wrong and why the customer had selected the competitor company as the preferred supplier. Technically and financially, there had been little to differentiate between the two sales packages. Finally, an armed forces liaison officer in the country was advised by a local defence department civil servant that the general feeling was that the company had 'sent a boy to do a man's job'. Western culture is often criticised for its 'cult of youth', where in certain fields, executives are considered 'past it' as early as their 40s. In many Eastern cultures, the exact opposite is often the case, and age is associated with accrued wisdom and life experience. The potential customer therefore found the company's reliance on such a 'boy wonder' quite disturbing, if not insulting, and this seriously inhibited their ability to draw any significant positives from the campaign he was heading up. In other words, they closed down their channels of communication and switched off. No sale.

The company that won the contract had brought back a key senior executive from early retirement to head up its campaign. He had successfully done business in that Far Eastern country before, and was well-respected there.

The obvious lesson from all this is that cultural differences really do matter. In university terms, what suits or even delights a fresher may make a mature student cringe – and vice versa. We need to be flexible in our responses to our customers, and to always try to tailor those responses accordingly.

'Know your customer' means just that. Know and understand their expectations, and know about any cultural issues that may affect how you can best deliver what they need. Finally, taking a leaf from the 'competitor's' book above, if you have someone who can bring some special skills or personal attributes to bear which could be instrumental in delivering exceptional customer care in a particular setting – for goodness sake use them! This not only maximises your ability to deliver top-quality service to your customer, but also gives that special 'someone' a personally rewarding opportunity to succeed, where perhaps, no-one else could. This is truly 'win-win' for all concerned.

Aim 3: To recognise from whom we receive service in general

The customer service chain

For any service to be successful, the staff must work well together and think positively of themselves and each other. We need to make it easier for our colleagues to help customers. In Chapter 9, we will discuss the OK Corral, and I'm OK, you're OK life positions – this is all about feeling good about ourselves and about our colleagues.

As a taster, consider the 'I'M OK' mnemonic:

- *Image* – you are representing the organisation so take care that your image is appropriate.

- *Mood* – when dealing with customers, moods should be left behind. You should never react badly to a customer or let them 'get to you'. Keep stress at bay by concentrating on your role, not on your problems. Talk over problems with colleagues or with family members. Interacting with people can be hard work.

- *On the ball* – always be ready to interact with customers. Don't get caught out.

- *Knowledge* of your job and the service so customers can be satisfied and cared for easily.

In summary, enjoy your work. Believe in yourself, your colleagues, the organisation and the service you are providing.

Remember: customer care is about being able to 'walk in the customer's shoes' and say you'd be happy to be treated the same way and to the same standards. Consider the following personal customer service checklist, and ask yourself whether you:

- arrive on time and fulfil your commitments to others;
- know and provide services effectively;
- know and help your colleagues;
- put personal problems aside;
- care for yourself, your health, appearance and personal hygiene;
- show a genuine desire to go out of your way to help customers;
- work with a positive attitude;
- always welcome customers appropriately;
- know your job well;
- know the organisational/departmental customer care standards;
- keep your work environment in good condition and assess this regularly;
- know how to use equipment when helping customers;
- give your best throughout your working hours;
- try not to let down the organisation, whether inside or outside work;

- walk in your customers' shoes to check your customer service;
- know you would be happy with your performance if you were your customer.

Aim 4: To recognise our internal customers

As well as external users of our services, a customer can be anyone in the organisation who benefits from the work that we do. This can include colleagues within our department or people in other parts of the organisation. We call these *internal customers*.

Like external customers, internal customers have requirements, and our processes often rely on a network of internal supplier and customer relationships in order to provide services to our customers. In a library, for example, such a chain can be found from acquisitions through cataloguing to circulation.

Positive internal customer relationships are a critical aspect of wider customer service because everybody in the organisation either directly serves external customers or helps colleagues who help external customers. Indeed, in one way or another, an organisation's staff members are all each other's internal customers, so it is essential that everyone contributes to the quality of customer service by maintaining the customer service chain. Recognising the existence of this chain and the importance of focusing efforts towards meeting the requirements of our internal customers within the chain is a powerful stimulus in getting things right, in improving our own work, and ultimately in satisfying our external customers.

We need to agree acceptable performance standards to meet the changing needs of our internal and external customers and to be responsive to changes as the need arises.

Service to and from

This exercise illustrates how in our daily lives we both give and receive service. Participants should draw up two lists, one headed 'service to', the other 'service from'. In the first list, participants should identify people or units to whom they give service, considering all the customers they serve in their working lives. In the other list, participants should identify people or units from whom they receive service in their working lives.

| Table 4.3 | Sample responses to the 'service to' and 'service from' activity |

I give service to	I receive service from
Home students	Student services
International students	Personnel services/human resources
Part-time students	Estates department
Distance learners	Wages department/finance
Our staff	Cleaners, janitors
My colleagues	Catering and food services
Anyone we meet in working day	Trade union
Other libraries	Leisure department of local authority
Members of the general public	Postal service
Telephone enquirers	Colleagues, administrators, technicians etc
Users with special needs	Staff training & development section
External consultants/researchers	Local authority

While the two lists decribe participants as individuals, when considered together it is possible for participants to see linkages with other individuals and departments. These linkages demonstrate our interdependence and our need to work as a team (we discuss teambuilding in Chapter 11).

Table 4.3 provides sample responses to this activity from a real-life customer care course run by the authors. Facilitators may find this useful to prompt participants.

Further reading

Abram, S. (2007) 'The future of reference in special libraries is what information pros can make it; If we sit and do nothing, we'll be like the frog in the pot: we won't know we're cooked until it's too late to jump', *Information Outlook*, October, available at: *http://findarticles.com/p/articles/mi_m0FWE/is_10_11/ai_n27424191/* (accessed 22 September 2009).

Alryalat, H. and Al Hawari, S. (2008) 'Towards customer knowledge relationship management: integrating knowledge management and customer relationship management process', *Journal of Information & Knowledge Management* 7 (3): 145–57.

American Library Association (2005) 'Guidelines for university library services to undergraduate students', available at: *http://www.ala.org/ala/mgrps/divs/acrl/standards/ulsundergraduate.cfm* (accessed 3 October 2009).

Barr, B., Conley, J. and Goode, J. (2003) 'Chat is now: administrative issues', *Internet Reference Services Quarterly* 8 (1/2): 19–25.

Bebko, C. P., Sciulli, L. M. and Garg, R. J. (2006) 'Consumers' level of expectation for services and the role of implicit service promises', *Services Marketing Quarterly* 28(2): 1–23.

Boyd, F .J. (1997) 'The customer may be always right – but who is the customer?' *Records Management Quarterly* 31(2): 38–44.

Broady-Preston, J. and Felice, J. (2006) 'Customers, relationships and libraries: University of Malta – a case study', *Aslib Proceedings* 58(6): 525–36.

Burwell, B. and Jones, R. (2005) 'Libraries and their service portfolios', *Searcher: The Magazine for Database Professionals* 13(6): 32–7.

Canadian Library Association (2000) 'Canadian guidelines on library and information services for older adults', available at: *http://www.cla.ca/AM/Template.cfm?Section=Position_Statements&Template=/CM/Content Display.cfm&ContentID=3029* (accessed 3 October 2009).

Canadian Library Association (1997) 'Canadian guidelines on library and information services for people with disabilities', available at: *http://www.cla.ca/AM/Template.cfm?Section=Position_Statements&Template=/CM/ContentDisplay.cfm&ContentID=4065* (accessed 3 October 2009).

Crossman-Miranda, J. (2007) 'Customer service skills for culturally diverse communities', available at: *http://infopeople.org/training/past/2007/diverse/* (accessed 25 September 2009).

Estes, M. E. (2000) 'Law librarians in the future', *Trends in Law Library Management & Technology* 11(1): 5–6.

Hahn, J. (2005) 'The techniques and benefits of observation inspired customer service', *Library Mosaics* 16(4): 14.

Hasty, D. F. (2004) 'Applying fourth generation management to access services: reinventing customer service and process management', *Journal of Access Services* 2(3): 21–42.

Herrera, K. and Herrera, G. (2007) 'Around the world: sushi and sweet tea at the University of Mississippi', *Library HI TECH News* 24(5): 16–19.

IFLA (2006) 'Guidelines for library services to babies and toddlers', available at: *http://archive.ifla.org/VII/d3/pub/Profrep100.pdf* (accessed 3 October 2009).

Rockman, I. F. (2004) 'Reaching in', *Reference Services Review* 32(2): 101–2.

Sullivan, M. (2004) 'The promise of appreciative inquiry in library organizations', *Library Trends*, 53(1): 218–29.

Williams, J. (2007) 'Are we asking the right questions?', *Texas Library Journal* 83(4): 148–9.

Wishnack, S. (year unknown) 'Providing meaningful and memorable customer service: Here's a road map to making it happen', available at: *http://www.thinkanddo.us/news.html* (accessed 20 September 2009).

Woodward, J. (2009) *Creating the Customer-Driven Academic Library*, Chicago, IL: American Library Association.

Wright, J. (2009) 'Sushi in the library', *The Paducah Sun (Kentucky)*, 16 March, available at: *http://www.paducahsun.com/component/content/article/183-archive/285908-* (accessed 3 February 2010).

5

Communication

I have often regretted my speech – never my silence. (Xenocrates)

The most important thing in communication is hearing what isn't said. (Peter F. Drucker)

Aims

The aims of this chapter are as follows:

- to recognise the barriers to communication;
- to recognise the importance of body language or non-verbal communication when dealing with customers face to face;
- to improve communications, whether face to face, over the telephone or in writing.

To assist with session planning, Table 5.1 presents a suggested session plan.

Background

Customers' first impressions can make or break a service, but reception personnel can, at times, be unhelpful, obstructive or even downright rude.

We have probably all experienced the feeling of being 'stone-walled' by a doctor's or dentist's receptionist. Many of us will also have approached a so-called 'welcome desk' only to be confronted by the most unwelcoming looking person in the organisation. This is unfortunate, because an organisation and/or an individual has but one opportunity to make the all-important first impression, and the mere absence of a smile can be enough to waste such an opportunity.

Table 5.1   Session plan – communication

Session	Aims	Content	Methods	Aids	Time (mins)
Communication	To recognise the barriers to communication		T		5
		Barriers to communication	A	F/C	10
	To recognise the importance of body language or NVC when dealing with customers face to face		T		5
		Body postures	A	H/O	10
	To improve communications whether face to face, in writing or on the phone		T		5
		E-mail communications	A	H/O	15
Approx. total time (mins)					50

*A, activity (participants); F/C, flipchart; H/O, handout; P/I, Post-it notes; T, talk (facilitator)

Customers can make judgments about a service in seconds, so it behoves us to get it right first time. It is not so much what you say but the way you say it. A whole world of meaning can be conveyed by the way you stand, how you regard people, and by your demeanour. Body language or non-verbal communication (NVC) is therefore of vital importance. Kowalsky (2006) describes how through NVC, such as folding their arms or rolling their eyes, service desk staff can appear disinclined to helping their customers and look like they would rather be elsewhere. In terms of verbal communication, Kowalsky mentions how sometimes reference librarians' first response to a customer enquiry is 'No...' and how such communications can impact negatively on customers.

In terms of the dynamics of communication, research shows that what is actually said accounts for only 7 per cent of what is initially taken in; paralinguistic features account for 38 per cent, while NVC contributes some 55 per cent to the equation.

By paralinguistic features, we mean tone, volume, pitch and rate of speaking. Tone, for example, can convey a mixed message, saying more about a speaker's true feelings than the actual words they are using. Volume can vary from being low (associated with timidity or sadness) to loud (associated with aggression or anger). Pitch or frequency can, for example, place emphasis on key words in a sentence, while rate can contribute to clarity, with slower speech being more intelligible and faster speech possibly conveying stress or anger.

Some body language experts believe that non-verbal cues account for 70–80 per cent of communication. However, an added complication is that the meanings of NVC can change around the world. Therefore, if you have many international customers, you need to be aware of international differences. The good news is that the smile is one universal aspect of NVC. Unfortunately, so is the frown.

Communication is a whole science in itself, so clearly one chapter of a book can only skim the surface of this complex topic, and focus on some key messages for customer service. Further chapters are devoted to specific aspects of communication – listening and questioning – to afford sufficient coverage to make readers/participants feel more confident in communicating with customers. If you find the topic particularly interesting, you may wish to pursue it further, and suggestions are made for additional reading in this area.

We have already stressed the importance of NVC. Communication is a process and therefore dynamic rather than static, in that it is occurring all the time. Non-communication is not an option. Even if you are on your own, you are communicating with yourself, trying to acquire meaning. When you interact with other people, you are transferring information through messages, by signs, by signals or non-verbal cues. In such an instance, you are the communicator, you have a message to send, you have a medium through which you are conveying the message, and that message is intended for a recipient (individual or group) from whom you get feedback in the form of a reaction indicating that the message has been received and understood – or perhaps even misunderstood.

As a communicator, when you are conveying information, you need to think and plan what you are trying to say, and the reason why you are saying it. You must then translate this into a form that makes sense to the recipient, so that they assign the intended meaning to your message. It is therefore important to use a vocabulary and sentence construction appropriate to your recipient. If your message has been successfully 'received and decoded', the recipient will give you feedback by making the expected/required response.

There are numerous communication media. This book focuses on those which you are most likely to use in interactions with your customers. In particular, this chapter focuses on the following four key media:

- *oral communication*: face to face;
- *oral communication*: telephone;
- *written communication*: e-mail, letter, fax;
- *non-verbal communication*: attitude, expression, posture.

Aim 1: To recognise the barriers to communication

Identifying barriers

For the first exercise, divide the participants into two groups. Probably the easiest way to do this is to number them 1 – 2 – 1 – 2 etc. then ask the '1s' to assemble to your left and the '2s' to assemble to your right. Then ask each group to think of barriers to communication, i.e. what can stop information getting through, and to make a list of these. It is probably simplest if you, as facilitator, write up the responses on a flipchart. Get one answer from the '1s' then a second answer from the '2s', then turn and turn about to ensure fairness.

To prompt or categorise responses, it may be worth classifying them as 'physical', 'mechanical', 'mental' and 'cultural'. The following list gives some answers given by a mixed group of library staff during a customer care session run by one of the authors:

- *Physical*:
  - impaired hearing;
  - speech impediments;
  - note-taking/distracting gestures.
- *Mechanical*:
  - poor acoustics;
  - breakdown of equipment, e.g. telephone, microphone, PA system, computers;
  - placement of equipment on a counter, table or desk between you and the customer equates to a barrier;

- layout and design of building, signs, notice boards etc.;
- note-taking.
- *Mental*:
  - attitude;
  - anger;
  - shyness;
  - stubbornness;
  - incompetence;
  - lack of concentration;
  - lack of understanding;
  - lack of knowledge;
  - lack of training;
  - hostile body language, e.g. defensiveness, arm-folding.
- *Cultural*:
  - language barrier;
  - regional accents/dialect;
  - jargon/technical language;
  - positioning/proximity;
  - lack of eye contact.

This list is by no means exhaustive – your group may well think of more. You may be surprised at the number of NVC barriers out there. It is, unfortunately, all too easy for staff confronted with the same customer question for the *n*th time to say one thing verbally while their facial expression, tone of voice and body language are giving a different message altogether. Try to get across the importance of viewing apparently naive, obvious requests as a positive chance to educate and to empower customers. If you are prepared to spend a little extra time explaining things, this will go a long way towards educating the customer and will save time/disputes in the future.

Another important area identified here is our tendency to use jargon or technical language. Many words and phrases that are commonplace to us are part of our professional or organisational culture and may be totally alien to our customers. Some staff may feel that use of such terms impresses customers, but their usage in a customer-focused context can seem supercilious or pompous. We want to impress customers with our attitude rather than our extensive technical vocabulary. However insignificant the customer's perceived problem may seem to us, by engaging with the issue and treating customers sensitively and with respect, we increase their confidence in us and open the lines of communication.

Some examples of jargon or technical terms that may require explanation are given below:

- address (form of address, e.g. Mr, Dr, Ms; postal address);
- article;
- audio-visual;
- call number;
- carrel;
- cart;
- catalogue;
- check in;
- check out;
- circulation;
- class number;
- closed access;
- corporate body;
- cross-reference;
- family name;
- fine;
- folio;
- forename/first name (do not use 'Christian name');
- fortnight;
- foyer;
- hold;
- inter-library loan;
- issue;
- journal;
- loan period;
- lobby;

- location;
- monograph;
- online public access catalogue (OPAC);
- overdue;
- periodical;
- quick reference;
- quiet discussion only (notice);
- recall;
- renew;
- reserve;
- return;
- serial;
- short loan;
- stack;
- strict silence (notice);
- surname;
- terminal;
- VDU.

You will probably have others specific to your own organisation. Consider any that may bemuse your customers and impose a barrier between you and them.

Aim 2: To recognise the importance of body language or NVC when dealing with customers face to face

Rapport with your customers can be improved through NVC. Your own body language can say much about your professional image and about the degree of respect you have for your customer. The last thing you want to do is to appear uninterested or irritated. Try to read your customers' NVC as regards their wishes and expectations and remember to be aware of their needs for personal space. Consider the following guidelines for personal space distances:

- *intimate – people with whom we have a loving/intimate relationship*: <45 cm (<18 in);

- *personal – close friends in an informal situation*: 45–120 cm (18–48 in);

- *social – customers, strangers, casual acquaintances*: 1.2–3.6 m (4–12 ft);

- *public – talking to groups*: >3.6 m (>12 ft).

Proximity is a cultural thing and sometimes you or the customer may feel that your personal space is being invaded. In the UK, USA, parts of Northern Europe and the Far East, a non-threatening distance would be as per the social category in the above list. In Latin America, Southern Europe, the Arab world and Africa, however, a non-threatening distance may well encroach what we Northern Europeans consider to be our personal or even intimate space. People in the latter group are being perfectly respectful according to their own culture, but may seem threatening or over-familiar to people in the former group.

As a further example of cultural respect, male staff dealing with strict Muslim women customers should be very formal, avoid looking directly at them and keep their distance.

Notable differences can even be found within broadly similar Northern European cultures. For example, on his first visit to Sweden, one of the present authors stopped for a drink in a bustling hotel bar, only to feel that he was being aggressively 'crowded out'. It was only when a more travelled colleague pointed to the Swedish customers quite happily bumping into each other and simply moving on, that he realised that the bumping and jostling was nothing personal.

Anyone who has seen the commercials produced by HSBC will be aware of how the same gesture can mean different things in different cultures. Many gestures are best avoided, especially pointing, beckoning or indicating numbers using your fingers.

Eye contact can also be a minefield. While in Western cultures looking someone straight in the eye is seen as indicating attentiveness, openness and honesty, in Eastern cultures this can be regarded as impolite and the listening response can be to look away from the speaker.

Mirroring or subtlety mimicking your customer's posture or movements can be a useful device when trying to put someone at ease.

Don't jump to the conclusion that your customer's every movement is a definitive sign of how they are feeling: remember the 'sign of four' rule, and try to find four NVC indicators signifying a similar mindset.

There are also NVC aspects to speech. The fact that someone is speaking very quickly does not always indicate anxiety, and loud or harsh vocal sounds do not always indicate aggression. When talking to international customers, think before you speak. Use simple language and short, direct sentences; speak fairly slowly (but don't labour this) and clearly. Avoid slang, jargon and dialect. Don't speak particularly loudly. Make general conversation for a minute or so to attune your ear to speech rhythms. You can attune your ear further by unobtrusive 'eavesdropping' on international customers talking among themselves.

Make allowances for cultural and behavioural differences. Apparently rude or aggressive behaviour is rarely intended, so don't immediately react as if it is. Remember also that some international customers may be overly polite and agreeable rather than indicate that they are experiencing difficulties or don't understand something. Bear in mind that any signals that you are giving off are also subject to misinterpretation or misunderstanding.

Where you deem international customers' behaviour unacceptable, don't react angrily or aggressively. Explain in a quiet, friendly but persistent way that this is not the way things are done here. Check that the customer really does understand the situation by making your meaning clear and unambiguous.

Remember PACIFIC:

- *P*ersevering
- *A*ssertive
- *C*alm
- *I*nterceding (e.g. negotiating)
- *F*riendly (but firm)
- *I*mperturbable
- *C*onfident

Chapter 9 will contain more advice regarding assertiveness and confidence.

Identifying non-verbal communication

You may wish to get participants to identify types of NVC. Alternatively, you may prefer to distribute the following list or to write the details onto a flipchart or whiteboard.

Consciously or unconsciously, when we speak we will also communicate by means of:

- *facial expression*: a smile, a frown;
- *gestures*: movement of hands and body to help explain or emphasise our verbal message;

- *body posture*: how we stand or sit;
- *orientation*: whether we face the other person or not;
- *eye contact*: whether we look at the other person or not, and the length of time that we look at the other person;
- *body contact*: a pat on the back, an arm on the shoulder;
- *proximity*: the distance we stand or sit from a person;
- *head nods/shakes*: to indicate agreement or disagreement or to encourage the other to go on speaking – or to stop.

It is essential to remember that NVC can be very powerful – the receiver will use these clues to interpret what you mean. If, for example, you are angry but are trying to hide your anger, you must be aware of your body posture, the way you use your eyes, gestures and facial expressions, and the tone of your voice, all of which may give you away.

Body postures

For this activity, participants are given a list of terms describing body postures. The facilitators may also wish to give them a handout of stick-men body postures, as shown in Figure 5.1. These are deliberately simple so that facilitators can easily replicate them by hand on a flipchart or whiteboard.

Participants are asked to decide which of the following terms best describe each of the body posture pictures:

- aloof;
- angry;
- ashamed;
- casual;
- descriptive;
- disinterested;
- dominating;
- doubtful;
- impatient;
- modest;
- questioning;
- resigned;
- sad;
- self-conscious;

Figure 5.1 Body postures

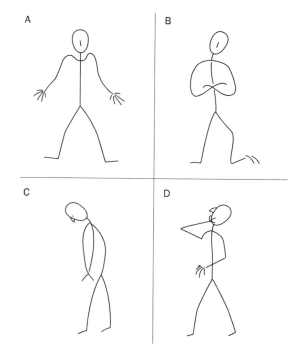

- self-satisfied;
- shy;
- surprised;
- suspicious;
- undecided.

The answers are as follows:

- *Posture A*
  - disinterested
  - descriptive
  - resigned
  - doubtful
  - questioning
- *Posture B*
  - angry

- casual
- descriptive
- impatient
- self-satisfied
- *Posture C*
  - ashamed
  - modest
  - sad
  - self-conscious
  - shy
- *Posture D*
  - aloof
  - dominating
  - surprised
  - suspicious
  - undecided

Depending how confident and uninhibited they feel, some facilitators might prefer to actually adopt some of the postures/gestures and ask the participants how they would interpret them. Table 5.2 gives a brief guide to some typical postures/gestures and their interpretation.

Table 5.2 Interpretation of postures and gestures

Posture/gesture	Interpretation
Brisk, erect walk	Confidence
Walking with hands in pockets, hunched shoulders	Dejection
Slumped posture	Low spirits, fatigue, feeling of inferiority
Erect posture	Confidence, high spirits
Relaxed posture	Openness
Rigid posture	Defensive
Standing with hands on hips	Readiness, aggression
Sitting with legs crossed, foot kicking slightly	Boredom
Sitting with legs apart	Openness, relaxed
Sitting with locked ankles	Apprehension

Table 5.2 Interpretation of postures and gestures (*Cont'd*)

Posture/gesture	Interpretation
Sitting with hands clasped behind head, legs crossed	Confidence, superiority
Sitting with crossed arms/legs	Defensive
Sitting with uncrossed arms/legs	Willingness to listen
Leaning forward	Open, interested
Leaning away	Defensive, uninterested
Looking down, face turned away	Disbelief
Head resting in hand, eyes downcast	Boredom
Quickly tilted head	Interest
Prolonged tilted head	Boredom
Hands clasped behind back	Anger, frustration, apprehension
Rubbing hands	Anticipation
Open palm	Sincerity, openness, innocence
Tapping or drumming fingers	Impatience
Steepling fingers	Authoritative
Biting nails	Insecurity, nervousness
Patting/fondling hair	Lack of self-confidence, insecurity
Hand to cheek	Evaluation, thinking
Rubbing the eye	Doubt, disbelief
Rubbing/touching nose slightly	Rejection, doubt, lying
Pinching bridge of nose, eyes closed	Negative evaluation
Pulling/tugging at ear	Indecisiveness
Stroking chin	Trying to make a decision

Aim 3: To improve communications, whether face to face, over the telephone or in writing

Oral communication: face to face

We have already explained how feeling good about yourself, about the way you behave and the way you look, can have a positive knock-on effect on your customer and on their degree of satisfaction with the service you provide. We have also mentioned the importance of speaking clearly and slowly when dealing with customers and of using your knowledge of NVC to interpret customer feelings. Previous chapters have touched on customer expectations and perceived needs to which you may be required to respond in a manner that creates a rapport and seeks to achieve customer satisfaction while operating within established organisational procedures. Future chapters will help you enhance your listening skills in order to attend to what your customers are saying, and will help you to better understand transactions between you and your customers (Chapters 6 and 9).

We are assuming that you have good knowledge of the service you are offering and of the organisational policies and procedures surrounding your service. You should therefore be able to explain the services on offer to your customers clearly and concisely. Your knowledge should help you to anticipate the sorts of customer requests and information needs you are likely to encounter. This will help you to plan and to engage in face-to-face communication with your customers in a way that is focused, structured and directed. Future sections of the manual will help you to hone your listening and questioning skills to ensure you elicit the necessary information from your customers.

Table 5.3 contains phrases or words that may appear negative and, alongside these, phrases or words that convey the same meaning but in a more positive light. You may want to use these with your participants. You could give them the list from column one and ask them to come up with some positives to replace the phrases or words used.

Later on, we discuss handling complaints (Chapter 7) and dealing with challenging situations (Chapter 8), but it is worth bearing in mind that by using positive words and phrases we can sometimes prevent situations escalating into something more serious. Some phrases can also help direct your customer toward solutions so that they feel they have participated in decision-making, for example:

- What would you like me to do now?
- What do you think is a fair way to resolve this?
- What would you be happy with?
- Would you like me to direct you to someone else with whom you can discuss this?

Of course it won't always work and sometimes what started out as a 'conversation' can develop into a potential confrontation. Remember PACIFIC.

Don't lose control, don't be defensive, but don't accept abuse either.

Table 5.3   Negatives and positives

Negative	Positive
You are confusing me	I am confused
You must fill in this form	Will you please fill in this form?
Wait here	Would you mind waiting here?
What is your problem?	Please tell me what happened
It is policy	We do that to benefit you because...
You should not get upset	I understand that you are upset
Don't forget	Do remember
Don't hesitate	Feel free
Appointment	Meeting
Free	Complimentary
Discount	Saving
No	What we can do is...
No worries	Certainly
No problem	You're welcome
Hope	Trust
Problem	Challenge
Sorry	Apologies
Not bad	Pretty good
I don't know	I will find out/I will check
Facilities	Services
But	However
Sadly/unfortunately	As/because
I'll try to	I will
I'm afraid	The situation is
That is not my job	Let me find the right member of staff to help you
You're right, this is bad	I understand your frustrations
It is not my fault	Let me see what we can do about this
You want it by when?	I will try my best
I am busy	I will be with you in just a moment
Call back	I will call you back; can I just confirm your phone number?

Oral communication: telephone

Customer satisfaction during telephone communication depends on good feelings about the way the transaction has been handled combined with the features and benefits of the service on offer. As such transactions cannot entail any NVC, so the customer's perception of the transaction relies on other factors, namely vocal impact (such as your tone, on which 82 per cent of perception is based) and verbal impact (the actual words you use, on which 18 per cent of perception is based). This contrasts significantly with a face-to-face encounter, where only 38 per cent of perception is based on tone and 7 per cent on words, the other 55 per cent deriving from body language. In addition to forming a rapport based on vocal and verbal impact, you need to be skilful in your use of the phone system (e.g. be familiar with features such as transferring calls) and in accessing appropriate information to deal with your customer's query.

Most organisations have a preferred standard mode of greeting to employ when answering the phone. This usually involves answering within a certain number of rings (usually before the fourth) and stating the organisational name clearly. You may also be required to state your department and/or your own name. Customers prefer to have the name of the person with whom they are talking so that they can refer to you in any follow-up to the communication.

Because of the importance of vocal impact, many manuals on telephone skills recommend putting 'a smile in your voice'. If you imagine that you are answering a call from a close friend when you pick up the receiver and smile as if you were meeting them face to face, the chances are that you will sound pleasant and welcoming and you will be halfway to establishing rapport with the customer. With respect to verbal impact, take care in choosing words in order to reduce the risk of misunderstanding or ambiguity. Avoid using jargon – refer back to the abovementioned glossary for some terms that may cause confusion.

In terms of the balance between listening and talking, the conversation should start with you letting the customer talk for 80 per cent of the time. As there is no NVC to guide the customer, your concern regarding the service they are receiving must be clear from the tone of your voice. To allow for possible poor reception, ensure that any talking you do is clearly enunciated and fairly slow. Adapt your speech to meet your customer's needs. Even if you feel that the customer is rambling on, be patient, don't interrupt, and don't try to hurry them along.

Take care of words with the same sounds, e.g. F and S, B and V and M and N. Use the NATO alphabet in spelling any difficult names:

- Alpha
- Bravo
- Charlie
- Delta
- Foxtrot
- Golf
- Hotel
- India
- Juliet
- Kilo
- Lima
- Mike
- November
- Oscar
- Papa
- Quebec
- Romeo
- Sierra
- Tango
- Uniform
- Victor
- Whiskey
- X-ray
- Yankee
- Zulu

Be aware that your customer is paying for the cost of the call and that you should try to avoid delays. If you are accessing or processing relevant information during the call, ensure that you keep the customer informed about your actions (e.g. I am just checking your file, yes I have it now, just getting to the right section...). Apologise for any delays or if you have to put them on 'hold'. Ensure that you cannot be heard by them if you are discussing actions with colleagues. Time gets exaggerated on the phone and having to wait even ten seconds can feel like ten minutes to the person hanging on the other end of the line. If you feel you are going to keep them on hold for an overly long period, undertake to call them back and ensure that you do so. If you have to transfer the call, explain why and ask if your customer is happy to have that call transferred. If they are not, use the call-back procedure where you contact the appropriate section/team in your organisation and pass contact details to them to contact the customer – and ensure that they do so. Where possible and permissible within your organisation, take ownership of the customer's enquiry – follow through the liaison with other sections/teams and see through the problem. This can result in a great sense of achievement and job satisfaction for you, and service satisfaction for the customer.

When answering a colleague's phone, don't say they are not in yet, at lunch or have gone home, as the caller may interpret that your colleague is late for work, taking a long lunch break or even skiving off. It makes a more professional impression if you say that they are unavailable at present, and will call back – just make sure that they do.

The procedure for dealing with customer queries should be similar to that undertaken for other communication means, namely:

- listening closely and identifying customer needs;
- checking facts to ensure your understanding and the accuracy of any notes/details you may have taken down, especially telephone numbers;
- choosing the 'best fit' option from those available to meet their needs;
- summarising any agreed course of action.

You may or may not be in a job role that requires you to make outgoing calls to your customers. If you are, ensure that you assemble all the information you need prior to phoning your customer. In addition, note what you want to cover before you ring the customer; for example, jot down headings of the topics as an aide memoire. Make the customer aware of the purpose of your call as soon as you can, while observing the niceties of opening the conversation with a smile in your voice to establish rapport.

Some organisations make follow-up phone calls to ensure customers were satisfied with the service provided. If yours does not, could this be something worth considering?

Most organisations have procedures for taking messages for colleagues, often on pre-printed pads. Ideally, you will be familiar with these. Also remember it is, unfortunately, easier for customers to be abusive on the phone, so check out your organisation's guidelines for handling abusive calls. If you are a victim of 'phone rage', try to stay calm and listen to what the customer has to say. Anger tends to die down as people get their problem 'off their chest' and you may be able to correct any misunderstanding there and then. If the call is abusive or offensive, follow organisational policy.

Whether you are making or receiving the call, give it your undivided attention, listen carefully and try to sound interested.

Remember that telephone calls carry an increased risk of confidentiality breaches. Take care to ensure the caller is who they say they are.

Also remember that unless your call is being transmitted over a highly secure, protected line, you are potentially talking to the world. There are people out there listening to you – some work for government agencies, some do not – either way, be aware that what you may consider to be a 'private discussion' may well be anything but!

Written communications: e-mail, letters, faxes

Whenever possible, more personal contact, either face to face or via the telephone is preferable to written communication. Direct personal contact can save time while, without due care, the written word can easily be misinterpreted. Direct contact is also 'real time', and as such, provides an ongoing opportunity to correct, clarify or further develop your communication. Written communication is more of a 'snapshot', and carries with it the risk of unresolved misinterpretation. In addition, remember that communicating in written form creates a permanent record, which carries inherent risks and limitations that are less likely to apply to oral communications. Dates of written communications will be preserved and need to indicate that any time lapse between receipt of and response to the communication is acceptable as well as indicative of excellent customer service. Avoid the sort of insensitive approach you would not adopt in a face-to-face situation. As with oral communication, you need to use clear, concise language and take care with your style and tone. Remember the simple ABC of written communication:

- accuracy;
- brevity;
- clarity.

There are conventions for business letters, and your organisation may have its own guidelines for written communications. Generally the rules are to:

- open the communication in a positive manner to establish rapport;
- state the purpose of the communication at the outset;
- summarise the key points;
- indicate resultant proposed actions on your or the customer's part.

Systems often automatically produce and circulate correspondence such as overdue letters or reminders. You might like to revisit these and ask if the wording is appropriate, and if the contents are impersonal and perhaps subject to misinterpretation. If these automated messages are either inappropriate or even offensive, they may well undermine all the previous, carefully crafted personal correspondence you have taken such pains to produce. The recipient will not blame the computer – they will blame you.

One useful source of information is the Plain English Campaign (*http://www.plainenglishcampaign.co.uk*). This organisation offers free guides, such as 'How to write in plain English' (*http://www.plainenglish .co.uk/files/howto.pdf*) and 'The A to Z of alternative words' (*http://www .plainenglish.co.uk/files/alternative.pdf*).

A further resource is the Economist Style Guide (*http://www .economist.co.uk/research/StyleGuide/*). This covers such topics as unnecessary words, active vs. passive, jargon, journalese and slang and common solecisms.

Depending on your role, you may deal with correspondence from customers. If you do, ensure that you understand why they have written to you. Assess what outcome they anticipate. Consider which of your response options will lead to customer satisfaction without compromising organisational policies and procedures. Summarise the outcome and consequent actions in your response to them.

Honesty is the best policy and, if there is going to be a delay in the resolution of a customer problem, it is better to inform the customer so that they know in advance and can plan accordingly. If we are presented with a problem that is seemingly insoluble, it is best to communicate with the user and try to help them find a resolution by some other means. This is always a better option than joining the 'blame culture', suggesting that the fault lies with another part of the organisation, with systems, procedures or technologies. Always give the customer a realistic timescale.

On the other hand, being honest does not necessitate overburdening customers with information. Limit communication to the essentials rather than expecting customers to absorb a great deal of information at once. You can supplement information with other communications such as notices, instructions and leaflets. Before such media are foisted on the customers, they should be tested out on a few potential users to ensure that they are well-written, up to date and responsive to users' needs.

The following are instructions from a leaflet accompanying a juice-making machine, reproduced verbatim from the allegedly English version:

How to use

1. First, manufacture fruit juice, peels first each kind of vegetables (depilation), goes the nucleus, slivers can put in presses out size of spare the juice through.

2. Second, joins the power source plug the power source, presses the switch, the fruits and vegetables which prepares put in press out in the juice through, with advances the stick downward to press gently, then extracts the original taste and flavour, the beneficial health fresh vegetables fruit juice.

3. Each kind of meats muscle, the bone, the skin and so on removes, slivers the 2×2 cm block, then puts in according to each time the 150 g component stirs in the meat cup, covers stirs the meat cutter head, clockwise revolves threads up mutually.

4. Notes: When stirs the meat to discover the component excessively are many or has the muscle to entangle the cutting tool, causes the electricity turning point to reduce speed, should the engine off, the dump, readjust immediately the component or removes the muscle uses again.

5. It will grind the cup to be suitable grinds the powder for doing food. When use, each time presses the 150 g component to put in stirs in the meat cup, covers stirs the meat cutter head, clockwise revolves threads up mutually.

6. Notes: When grinds food discovery idle operation, namely the bit cannot bump into food should the engine off, the dump, mix immediately food the loose regrinding.

7. It acts according to various people's diet custom, slivers massive the vegetables, the section shape, each time puts in 150 g–200 g vegetables, joins the right amount cooled boiled water to stir in the big cup, then makes each kind of fresh vegetables thick liquid.

Given that these instructions are for an electrical appliance with blades and a grinding mechanism, there are obvious health and safety implications.

The example above provides a salutary lesson about the need for careful, accurate translation where original foreign language documents are concerned. As a final fail-safe measure, such translated documents should always be read and checked over for content and style by a native-speaker of the language concerned. Even the most highly-qualified translators can slip up occasionally – particularly where vernacular is concerned. The late President John F. Kennedy's staff infamously provided him with an apocryphal example of this when they prepared his speech for his visit to Berlin on 26 June 1963. His declaration: 'Ich bin ein Berliner' was met by a roar from the crowd which was misinterpreted as loud, vocal approval. It was in fact raucous laughter, prompted by the admission that he was a small, sugary doughnut ... a 'Berliner'. (Although this tale was printed in several 'quality' publications of the day, some more recent sources suggest that it may in fact be an urban myth. Whatever the truth of the matter, it remains a good story, and certainly underlines the dangers of ambiguity.)

One way in which it is common to over-communicate is with e-mail. We are all only too aware of the curse of 'spam'. It is easy to send global e-mails to customers, but overwhelming them with details or explanations which are irrelevant to them serves only to lessen the impact of this particular medium of communication.

Research by Transversal suggests that e-mail is the UK's worst channel for customer service, with only 46 per cent of routine customer service questions answered adequately. In addition, the Transversal study found the average e-mail response time to be 46 hours, with 28 per cent of the organisations surveyed failing to reply at all. However, given that some organisations responded with useful answers within ten minutes, effective use of e-mail in customer service is possible. Participants might like to consider how effectively it is used in their own organisations.

A recent development in communications has been social networking and the use of sites such as Facebook, Twitter, LinkedIn, YouTube and Flickr. These provide real-time updates and information-sharing, so have potential benefits for letting customers know about special events, giving customers useful information to help them make informed decisions, and gaining intelligence as regards customer preferences, for example.

Many libraries have realised the usefulness of engaging with their customers online, for example, Hampshire libraries have a Twitter presence for interested customers. The nature of Twitter means that people following their service have hundreds of 'followers' or fellow tweeters themselves, many with similar interests, who help to spread their message virtually. In the same county, the EDGE Project is a Hampshire Museums & Galleries Trust initiative that actively seeks to engage people aged 14–24 with Hampshire museums, galleries, libraries and discovery centres (*http://www.facebook.com/group.php?gid=20452130765*).

'Social network marketing' and 'social media marketing' are terms used to describe using media such as social networks, online communities, blogs or wikis for marketing, public relations and customer service. Participants may have examples of how they perceive social networking could be used for customer care purposes. Rogers (2009) describes how US libraries are using such media to access information to gain insight from customers.

Activity 1

Below are two e-mails, one from SF (internal customer) and a reply from LM.
    Participants are required to split into groups of three or four people to analyse the response below. They should prepare to give feedback about its appropriateness and any other comments they wish to make. How should this have been dealt with?

From: PG

Sent: 3 June 2009 11:56

To: LM

Subject: Travel arrangements for this week's trip to Portugal

L

I have just received my travel details and tickets for next week and, unfortunately, there appears to be some kind of mix-up. While all the accommodation that I require in Portugal has been booked, my internal train trip to Lisbon, which I did request, has not. I am due to start the trip in two days time, how can this problem be resolved?

Kind regards

PG

Researcher, Learning & Teaching Support

From: LM

Sent: 3 June 2009 11:58

To: PG

Subject:

Dear P

I passed the details on to CS who said she had made all the arrangements. She is not in today. I suggest that you either e-mail or call her tomorrow.

LM

Executive Team Assistant, Academic Registry

Activity 2

Below are two e-mails in letter format. One is from AB (the buildings insurance policy holder), and the reply is from CD, a member of staff working in the customer service department of the insurance company concerned. Again the participants are required to read both and then to analyse the response to the e-mail from CD.

The example above is based on a genuine incident, which was in fact referred to the Insurance Ombudsman. A cash award was made to the complainant, as the company concerned was found to have acted unprofessionally.

Customer Service Department

Apocalypse Insurance Company

Dear/Sir Madam,

I would like to formally bring the following matters to your urgent attention. When my mother passed away three months ago, as executor and sole beneficiary in her will, I inherited her bungalow. When probate was granted, I immediately advised you by e-mail that I wished to continue to insure the property through your company. You e-mailed by return and acknowledged that this was in hand. Reassured by this, I went on a pre-booked foreign holiday for two weeks, where I had no access to e-mail.

On my return, on checking my e-mail I was most distressed to discover that in my absence, your company had in fact declined to provide insurance cover for the property concerned, and that you had in fact unilaterally cancelled the policy, with no reference to me, with effect from 2nd December. This has meant that the property has in fact been uninsured for the past 12 days. Fortunately, no damage has occurred in our absence, and I have now been able to obtain alternative cover.

This has caused me considerable worry – and particularly in view of my recent bereavement this is stress that I could well do without. I am therefore advising you that I am considering referring this case to the Insurance Ombudsman as an example of unacceptable practice. I would be interested to hear from you as regards your further action in this matter.

Yours Sincerely

AB

Mrs AB

The Bungalow

Dear Mrs. AB,

The Company notes your comments and can only repeat that we choose not to insure second properties for new customers – which in effect you were following your mother's death. Furthermore, when we advised you that we were cancelling the policy cover we were not aware that you were abroad at the time, or of the fact that you had no access to e-mail.

Such cancellation is standard practice where the terms of the policy cannot be met as regards a particular property. You will find that this practice is commonly applied throughout the insurance industry.

Yours Sincerely

CD

Case study: 'Get connected'

We recently attempted to arrange a telephone and broadband connection for a property in a Southern European (EU) country (which shall remain nameless!) To initiate the process, we visited the local office of the company concerned (the main, national supplier). Our visit took place mid-morning, on a Thursday. The office was extremely well-appointed, air-conditioned and modern, with four separate service counters and two small 'interview' rooms for more private consultations. Despite the availability of multiple potential service points, only one was permanently staffed. When we joined the queue in front of this counter, there were already three other customers ahead of us.

The staff were all clearly identifiable as they were all wearing 'Telecom' polo shirts. In addition to the person manning the service point, two other staff-members were located in this front-office area. We have no idea how many staff there were in the offices at the rear, but this was a large, three-storey building.

The one member of staff who was covering a service point was very attentive and thorough, and quite rightly gave the impression that he would not be rushed into delivering poor results. Soon after we arrived, it became clear that the customer at the head of the queue had a rather complex requirement that involved the return of some defective equipment and the issue of a replacement item. By the time his customer needs had been satisfied (about 20 minutes), the queue had grown from three to seven customers.

At this stage, one of the unoccupied staff asked if anyone in the queue simply wanted to pay a bill, and if so, would they come to another counter, where she would deal with them. Two customers did this, and were then quickly on their way. She then returned to her conversation with the other, apparently unoccupied employee.

By the time we reached the counter, the queue had grown to nine customers, and the two 'unoccupied' staff were still deep in conversation. By this stage, the customer immediately behind us was clearly becoming frustrated – very telling body language with arms folded across his chest and foot tapping away – plus an aside to the room in general that it had 'been like this for the past five years'.

The sole member of staff who seemed to be 'customer-focused' dealt with us efficiently and courteously, and we went on our way with the advice that 'within two weeks' the company would be in touch to arrange a connection date.

Sure enough, 'within two weeks' the company called us – on a Friday evening at 9 pm – to advise that they would be connecting us on the following Monday morning, between 9.30 and 10.30 am. Unfortunately, we then received a call on the Saturday evening to say that the original connection date could no longer be met. However, the company would call us back 'within 48 hours' to arrange a connection date and time.

After 72 hours had passed with no contact from the company, we called them. No apology was offered, and we were asked to wait on hold while the requirement was checked out. After a fruitless wait of some ten minutes, during which time we were transferred to three different operators, we were then advised that the problem could not be resolved immediately, but that someone would call us back within 24 hours. In fact, we received a call less than an hour later, but only to advise us that it was not currently possible to confirm either a date or a time, as there were 'no free slots at present'. The company promised to call us back when a slot became available. On asking whether this would be within hours, days, or weeks, we were advised that it was impossible to say – but we would receive a call 'as soon as possible'.

Within two or three days, we then received a further telephone call on our mobile from the service provider, asking for someone with a local surname who had asked for his phone to be removed. We explained that we were not that person, and that there had clearly been a mix-up. The caller apologised, and said that they would contact the 'local operations manager' to establish what had happened to our requirement. Sure enough, we got another call the following day – unfortunately asking for the same 'mystery local' who wanted his line disconnecting. Further apologies were forthcoming, but still no news of connection.

A week later, with still no sign of progress, we visited the local office again. Once more, we were greeted with a long queue ahead of us, only one manned service point (three vacant), and two 'front of house' staff apparently still deep in personal conversation over the latest football scores – or similar. After a 45-minute wait, the basic problem was explained – the existing junction box was full, and a new one would have to be fitted outside our apartment. Normally, we were told, such work would be completed 'within two weeks', but regrettably this might not be possible due to the volume of employees on holiday.

Three weeks later, the connection was made, with both a telephone line into the apartment, and a wireless connection for our laptops. What we were originally advised would take two weeks to achieve, had in fact taken eight weeks, plus a number of frustrating visits to the local office in order to progress our requirement in person.

It was therefore a pleasant surprise that the after-installation service was excellent, with an English-speaking support engineer painstakingly talking us through every intricacy of establishing both an internet modem and a wireless connection. This is an interesting reversal of what can so often be the case, where once the initial sale has been made, the after-sales service is then either poor or non-existent.

Analysis

- It is not enough to create a comfortable, modern and attractive 'front of house' if you do not have the staff to run it efficiently – either because of poor training or sheer indifference.

- Customers will assume that *all* staff in the front-office area are both competent and available to deal with their customer needs. If this is not the case, the staff should not be there in the first place.

- To keep customers waiting in a queue for 20 minutes before making it clear that those who wish only to pay bills can be dealt with separately and quickly, shows scant regard for customer needs. This is poor communication, and indicates little or no interest in either identifying or meeting the customer requirement efficiently.

- In this example, the company concerned is the major national supplier, and unlike the UK telecom industry, has only limited competition. This is no excuse for complacency, or for adopting a 'take it or leave it' approach to customer care. Even sole suppliers should strive for excellent customer service.

- If you cannot meet a delivery promise, then don't make it in the first place. Failed delivery forecasts are a common source of customer frustration. If you have to give such a forecast, always err on the side of caution, and provide a date which you know you can meet, barring disasters. When your actual delivery then beats the forecast, the customer will be duly impressed with your efficiency.

- If you tell a customer that you will call them back within a certain timescale, make absolutely certain that you do so. Call them even if you have not yet solved their particular problem. An update on even limited progress is infinitely better than being ignored. If a customer has to call you because you have not contacted them as promised, don't expect them to be impressed.

- Get it right first time. For a customer to have to wait four weeks before they are advised what the actual reason for delay is, is simply unacceptable. The lack of available connection points should have been highlighted – if not on day one – then certainly soon after that.

Just for fun

For a bit of light relief, you might like to share with your participants this brief exercise on checking how well they receive communication. Just hand out the following three-minute test and ask them to do it.

1. Read everything before doing anything.
2. Write your name in the top left-hand corner of this sheet.
3. Underline your name.
4. Personalise this sheet with a small 'stick person' in the top right-hand corner.

5. Say your name out loud when you have reached this question.

6. Circle the word NAME in this sentence.

7. Put three ticks or check marks at the end of this sentence.

8. Put three crosses at the end of this sentence.

9. Put the signs for plus, minus, divided and times at the end of this sentence.

10. If you are getting bored with this test, say 'yes' out loud. If not, say 'no' aloud.

11. Multiply 56 × 8. You can use the right-hand margin to do this sum.

12. Circle the word 'sheet' where it occurs in the sentences above.

13. If you think you are following instructions well, say 'yes' out loud.

14. Write your birth date in the format dd/mm/yyyy.

15. Count down in your normal speaking voice from ten to zero.

16. Stand up, turn around, then sit down again.

17. Say, 'nearly finished'.

18. Say 'almost there'.

19. Say 'done' and put your pen down.

20. Now you have finished reading carefully, as instructed in sentence (1), do only what you are asked to do in sentence (2). Or have you already done it?

Are you one of those people who gets a new gizmo or gadget, opens it up and starts playing with it without recourse to the instructions? If, like me, you are, you were probably fooled by the above exercise.

Final comments

Communication is a two-way process and one important skill that customer service staff can develop is that of actively listening to customers. We can only support our customers if we have a thorough understanding of their needs, and proactive listening can give us such understanding. Listening is one of the subjects covered in Chapter 6. Another way of listening to our customers is to get feedback from them via surveys, questionnaires, complaints books or focus groups. This is covered in Chapter 10, on suggestions for improvement.

Further reading

Anonymous (2006) 'Creative customer care in Arbroath', *Information Scotland* 4(1): 6.

Anonymous (2008) 'E-mail black hole causing customer service crisis', *Managing Information* 15(2): 15–16.

Austin, L. (2006) 'Service with a smile', *Arkansas Libraries* 63(2): 18–19.

Economist (year unknown) 'The Economist style guide', available at: *http://www.economist.co.uk/research/StyleGuide/* (accessed 23 September 2009).

Ekman, P. (2009) *Emotions Revealed*, London: Orion.

Gannon-Leary, P. (1997) '"E" for exposed? E-mail and privacy issues', *Electronic Library* 15(3): 221–6.

Kowalsky, M. (2006) 'Hi! No, I can't help you...' *One-Person Library* 23(8): 11.

Lawton, E. (2006) *Body Language and the First Line Manager*, Oxford: Chandos.

Morris, D. (1977) *Manwatching: A Field Guide to Human Behaviour*, London: Cape.

Plain English Campaign, available at: *http://www.plainenglishcampaign.co.uk* (accessed 23 September 2009).

Rogers, C. R. (2009) 'Social media, libraries and Web 2.0: How American libraries are using new tools for public relations and to attract new users', paper presented at the 98th German Library Association Annual Conference Deutscher Bibliothekartag, Erfut, 2–5 June.

Sisselman, P. (2009) 'Exploiting the social style of patrons to improve their satisfaction with the reference interview', *Library Review* 58(2): 124–33.

Vargas, M. F. (1986) *Louder Than Words: Nonverbal Communication*, Ames, IA: Iowa State Press.

Yellin, E. (2008) *Your Call is (not that) Important to Us: Customer Service and What it Reveals about our World and our Lives*, New York: Free Press.

6

Questioning and active listening

I keep six honest serving-men,
(They taught me all I knew),
Their names are What and Why and When,
And How and Where and Who.
(Rudyard Kipling)

There is nothing so annoying as to have two people talking when you're busy interrupting. (Mark Twain)

Instead of listening to what is being said to them, many managers are already listening to what they are going to say. (Anon)

Aims

The aims of this chapter are as follows:

- to identify the different types of questions and their effect on communication;
- to use questions to communicate more effectively;
- to encourage more active and effective listening.

To assist with planning, Table 6.1 presents a suggested session plan.

Background

This chapter on questioning and listening follows on from the previous chapter on communication. We'll start this by posing two questions:

Table 6.1   Session plan – questioning and active listening

Session	Aims	Content	Methods	Aids	Time (mins)
Questioning and active listening	To identify the different types of questions and their effect on communication		T		10
		Questioning analysis	A	H/O	10
	To use questions to communicate more effectively				
		Percentages of time spent on activities including listening	T	F/C	5
	To encourage more active and effective listening	Chinese whispers	A		10
		I want to tell you a story...	A	H/O	10
Approx. total time (mins)					45

*A, activity (participants); F/C, flipchart; H/O, handout; P/I, Post-it notes; T, talk (facilitator)

- First, what is a question?
- Second, why do we ask questions?

The answers to both are fairly obvious. A question is something we ask someone else (in our case a customer) and the reason we ask questions is to gather information (from our customers, preferably in a structured way).

Good questioning skills are an essential part of customer service and your aim should be to develop a constructive questioning approach. Failure to ask the right questions will result in failure to elicit the information you need to know. The quantity and quality of information collected will be dependent on your ability to come up with appropriate questions and to ask them in such a way that they elicit the desired information.

Developing an ability to question customers constructively requires an understanding of the different types of questions that can be used, as well as the types of response that the different types of questions are likely to elicit.

Successful adoption of a constructive questioning approach requires you to be clear about what you wish to achieve in asking your questions so that you ask the 'right' ones. You then need to be able to accurately assess the information gleaned from your questioning, to make decisions based on the information and follow through with the appropriate course of action.

The exercises on questioning help participants to understand the types of questions available so that they can be prepared to ask an appropriate question or mix of questions to elicit the quantity and quality of information required.

Bear in mind what was said in the previous chapter about avoiding jargon or technical language and about using appropriate language to match your customer. Listening (which will be covered later in this chapter) is obviously vital because you need to take on board your customer's responses to your question(s) prior to framing your follow-up question(s).

Aim 1: To identify the different types of questions and their effect on communication

There are eight different types of questions:

- *closed*: these tend to involve a limited, yes/no or one-word response;

- *open*: these require more than a yes/no or one-word response;

- *probing*: these try to dig more deeply into what the customer is asking;

- *bridging/linking*: these combine two concepts or ideas in one/two questions;

- *reflective*: these echo some of the customer's line of questioning and create thinking time;

- *summarising*: these recap the question along with your response to ensure understanding;

- *leading*: these require more than a yes/no or one-word response, but contain within them an indication of the response you expect to receive;

- *multiple*: this type of question can be complex or confusing as it asks more than one question simultaneously.

There are four key skills to handling customer questions:

- taking notes (suitable if you have a customer question over the phone, but a potential barrier to communication in face-to-face encounters);
- effective listening (covered later);
- effective questioning (this chapter);
- summarising (this can include follow-up questions and then checking understanding with the customer).

Questioning analysis

The following exercise requires the participants to work in pairs to analyse the questions given in Table 6.2 and work out what kinds of questions are being asked, based on the previously discussed list of question types. This can be quite difficult, as some of the questions represent multiple question types, so clarify the answers after the exercise by sharing the information given in the final column.

Table 6.2   Types of question

No.	Question	Type
1	How are things?	Open question requiring fact and opinion. Useful for establishing rapport at the outset of a transaction.
2	What was the traffic like on your journey here this morning?	Open question requiring fact and opinion. Useful for establishing rapport at the outset of a transaction.
3	What is this concern you have about database errors? How much extra would you consider paying to eliminate them?	Open question requiring fact, opinion and suggestions. Useful for opening up a particular topic.
4	What ideas do you have about how the library might position itself for continuous growth?	Open question requiring fact, opinion and suggestions. Useful for opening up a particular topic.
5	What is your attitude towards dealing with an increasingly diverse customer population?	Open question seeking opinion. Useful to discover the feelings of customers/ colleagues.

Table 6.2 Types of question (*Cont'd*)

No.	Question	Type
6	How do you feel about allowing customers to eat and drink in the library?	Open question seeking opinion. Useful to discover the feelings of customers/colleagues.
7	If you could produce a wish list for your organisation for the next five years, what would your top three wishes be?	Open seeking suggestions. Useful to gain insight. You are asking for three so it could be partially construed as closed but probing to elicit more information for the choices would counteract this.
8	How long have you worked for the organisation?	Closed requiring fact. Useful for collecting very specific pieces of information.
9	When did you arrive at work this morning?	Closed requiring fact. Useful for collecting very specific pieces of information.
10	Do you have your library card?	Closed requiring facts – possibly just a yes/no answer. Useful to gain precise information.
11	Do you know your library barcode number?	Closed requiring facts. Useful to gain precise information such as a number.
12	Ah, so you have worked here for ten years now. How has your job changed over that time?	Probing for more facts. Useful to demonstrate an interest in the customer/colleague and to encourage them to continue talking and give you further information.
13	If I have heard you correctly, you are saying you are frustrated at work. Are you given freedom to make your own decisions about the procedures you use to do your job?	Probing/leading. Restates facts given and requests more of the same but in this case may be assuming reasons for frustration. Useful to confirm your understanding on information gathered so far.
14	You feel that customers are more demanding than they were five years ago. What evidence do you have to support this contention?	Probing/bridging/linking trying to elicit more facts and opinions to increase the quantity and quality of information gathered. Questions like this need to be posed carefully. Tone of voice needs modification so that it does not come across as overly critical.
15	I gather you had a problem using the self-check out system. Can you tell me more about what happened, please?	Probing/bridging/linking trying to clarify or elaborate on the information gleaned from the customer. Again, tone of voice is important, as is avoidance of lapsing into any jargon or technical language.

Table 6.2 Types of question (*Cont'd*)

No.	Question	Type
16	You say that a customer was aggressive towards you. Why do you say that?	Probing/bridging/linking to elicit more facts and opinions and to supplement the information collected so far. This is another one where tone of voice is important as you don't want to come across as confrontational.
17	So, how you see it is as follows ... the qualities you would look for when hiring a library assistant include literacy, numeracy, good interpersonal skills...?	Summarising/reflecting to confirm your own understanding of the information given by the colleague/customer so far. Useful for restating facts and opinions and for eliciting further facts, opinions and suggestions.
18	What is your opinion of our organisation's customer service?	Open. This is a relatively unstructured question so gives the customer/colleague an opportunity to go in whatever direction they wish.
19	As a customer of our organisation, what sort of service(s) do you make most use of and why?	Open/multiple/leading. This is more structured than the question above, as it leads the customer towards a particular type of response. This is similar to a sentence completion statement in a questionnaire but it also contains more than one sentence as it asks not only 'what' but 'why'.
20	So the organisation is expanding rapidly at the moment. How will you keep close to customers?	Probing/bridging/linking to elicit opinions and suggestions.
21	You say you find it rewarding to work for this organisation. You have given some reasons. Is there anything else you would like to add?	Probing/bridging/linking to elicit elaboration.
22	Your job title is technical services assistant. Could you explain your role in a little more detail please?	Probing/bridging/linking to elicit clarification.

Table 6.2   Types of question *(Cont'd)*

No.	Question	Type
23	Can you tell me more about how your working day is made up?	Probing to increase the quality and quantity of information collected, especially factual information rather than opinions or suggestions.
24	What led you to think that our opening hours had been changed?	Probing to increase the quality and quantity of information. In this case, tone of voice is important as you don't want to come across as challenging or criticising the customer.
25	If you are unable to borrow the item, have you considered any of the alternatives – photocopying relevant sections, scanning text, borrowing a copy via interlibrary loan...?	Probing/leading to prompt the customer to come up with solutions.

Aim 2: To use questions to communicate more effectively

Questions invite customers to talk and should demonstrate that we are listening to them. We use probing questions to clarify their comments and, in so doing, confirm that we have listened to what they said. By using bridging or linking questions, we can confirm that we have assimilated the information they provided.

Aim 3: To encourage more active and effective listening

Having discussed questioning, we now move on to discuss active listening. Knowing how to listen actively is crucial in customer relationships. Unless you possess good listening skills you will be unable to receive the information you need to take action. Careful listening can reveal hitherto unidentified problems, highlight opportunities, and result in creative problem solving. It is actually quite hard to listen effectively, yet it is not part of our formal training in school – we learn how to read and write, but not necessarily how to listen.

Listening is something people tend to take for granted because they confuse it with hearing. Listening is much more than just hearing as the listener has to find meaning in what the customer is saying to them and to make sense of what they are trying to communicate. The process could be represented by the following formula:

active listening = hearing + finding meaning + making sense

To aid in finding meaning and making sense, the listener makes a conscious effort to check that their understanding tallies with the intended message of the customer. Summarising, probing or bridging/linking questions, as described previously, help in this process.

People are often described in flattering terms as being 'a good listener', and this skill can help build solid working relationships. All too often, people are more concerned with what they want to get across rather than with listening to what the customer is saying. The more time you spend talking, the less time the customer gets to talk to you, and you may be seen as dodging the issue in hand.

If you pause for breath, giving the customer a chance to get a word in edgewise, you may then start thinking about what you are going to say when you resume talking, rather than actively listening to what they have to say. Poor listeners often use the time when their customers are speaking as thinking time for themselves, a chance to regroup, possibly even to think up a suitable rejoinder. Some poor listeners also nod their head occasionally while doing this just to try to give the impression of paying attention, but the glazed look in their eyes can give them away. Inability or reluctance to afford sufficient attention to the customer will inhibit active listening, as will interrupting – and finishing customers' sentences for them.

Observation of non-verbal communication (discussed in the previous chapter) is also part of active listening. During the process, you need to be aware of both the customer's tone of voice and their body language, as these will be indicative of their emotional state.

There are ways in which the ability to listen can be improved. Before this, however, facilitators are invited to engage the participants in two exercises to test their listening skills.

Time spent on activities

First, ask the participants to consider their current job roles, and the percentage of their time they spend on the following activities:

- writing;
- reading;
- speaking;
- listening.

You don't need to spend overlong on this activity. Perhaps write the four activities on a flipchart or whiteboard then write down suggested percentages from the floor.

In fact, research indicates that the average office job breaks down as follows:

- *writing*: 9 per cent;
- *reading*: 16 per cent;
- *speaking*: 30 per cent;
- *listening*: 45 per cent.

Chinese whispers

For this exercise, the facilitator moves to the back of the room or even outside the room, depending on the acoustics. The first participant joins the facilitator who then whispers the following sentence to them:

> Meet Lena at 8 o'clock in the Borough, the bun fight is at 9 pm at Toscanini's.

The facilitator then returns to the front of the room and sends out the second participant. The first participant then whispers the sentence they heard to the second participant, then returns to the front of the room and sends out the third participant, and so on. This continues until every participant has been to the back of the room. The last participant is then asked to say (or write down) the sentence they heard.

Normally you will find that the original sentence has been changed out of all recognition. In one session we conducted, the sentence received by the final participant was, 'Cleaners in the garage will be through before the bonfire at Paganini's'!

I want to tell you a story...

For this activity, the facilitator is required to read out the following text twice. Participants are asked to listen carefully and can make notes if they wish. Having finished reading the story, the facilitator gives the participants a handout containing seven questions to answer. While participants are making notes, facilitators may wish to prepare a flipchart with the numbers one to seven before calling upon participants for their answers.

The text to be read aloud is as follows:

> Please ask your representative Alex Kennedy to meet Jack O'Malley from our head office at the bank at 12.30 pm. Mrs Walker from Quality Solutions will be waiting for them in the manager's office. Ask Alex to bring Mr O'Malley and Mrs Walker to our showroom at 59 Chancery Lane for a meeting at 2.30 pm. After this meeting, Mr Dalziel will decide whether to hold any further talks on the product launch.

The questions are as follows:

1. Who is going to the bank to meet someone?
2. What is the address of Quality Solutions?
3. Which company does Mr O'Malley work for?
4. Is there enough time to get to the meeting?
5. When does the meeting begin?
6. Who is the most senior person mentioned?
7. What is the purpose of the meeting?

The answers are as follows:

1. Alex Kennedy – although there is no indication whether Alex is male or female.
2. The address for Quality Solutions was not given – perhaps you remembered the only address given, which was 59 Chancery Lane.
3. No name was given – it referred only to head office.
4. It is difficult to answer this question, as no information is given on distances or how long the journey will take.
5. 2.30 pm.
6. There is not enough information to answer this. It could be Mr Dalziel as he is the decision maker but you can't assume this.
7. The purpose of the meeting is not stated. You may have made an assumption that it was to do with a product launch.

At the end of the exercise, ask participants to review their own scores. You will be lucky if you have any with a perfect seven. Ask them why so few were able to answer all the questions. You might like to record their responses on a flipchart. Remind participants that the exercise is designed to show how poor most of us are at listening.

Lessons from the activities

The above exercises illustrate the importance of listening to the *whole* message. The final exercise differs from customer service situations because there is less opportunity to ask for repetition of the whole thing. There is however, the opportunity to ask appropriate, clarifying questions.

In a work situation, listening can be restricted by a tendency to focus on particular types of information or particular parts of messages – in effect hearing only what we want to hear.

The exercises illustrate that it is relatively easy to gather concrete answers, such as names and times, but less easy to get the gist of the whole thing. In a customer service situation, we must listen, get a sense of what is said, consider what we have heard, and then make a response. It is quite demanding.

Your ability to actively listen can be improved. One way in which this can be done is to avoid labelling your customer. Unfortunately there is a tendency to pay more attention when listening to colleagues who are perceived as more senior and to customers who might be perceived as more 'important'. Some people tend to downgrade customers for whom English is a second language (Fayer and Krasinski 1987; Derwing et al. 2002) and such a negative attitude can result in decreased intelligibility.

Barriers to active listening include the following:

- *ears open, mind closed*: you are jumping to conclusions about what the customer is going to say next;

- *on again, off again*: you are thinking about what you are going to say next;

- *glazing over*: your mind has wandered onto matters other than your customer;

- *trigger*: you have heard a key word in the customer's sentence that has engendered an emotional response in you so you are putting up barriers or want to interrupt them;

- *look how actively I am listening*: you are trying too hard, repeating some of the facts the customer has given you and, in the process, missing new facts;

- *dodgeball*: you are avoiding the issue, failing to ask for clarification;

- *I'm ahead of you*: you have already decided on the outcome so have switched off;

- *hang on a minute*: you are being distracted by phone calls, noises in the corridor etc.

As we have said, active listening can be demanding, but don't get over-anxious about how you are going to respond. Breathe deeply and focus on what the customer is saying to help you to slow down and to take it all in rather than thinking about what they and you are going to say next. Try to tune into them using clues form their non-verbal communication (remember the 'sign of four' in Chapter 5 and try to find four indicators signifying a similar mindset); this will not only help you concentrate but will establish a rapport.

Don't jump the gun by trying to identify the issue before the customer has finished talking. Ask the right questions so that you get information that will help you not only to understand the customer's unfulfilled needs but will also help you make better decisions to help meet the needs of this customer – and others – in the future.

There is much literature on issues of cross-cultural communication and on problems experienced by library personnel when listening to international customers (Amsberry 2008). We have already mentioned trying to become attuned to the accents of international students (Sarkodie-Mensah 1992) and practising active listening (Kumar and Suresh, 2000; Curry and Copeman 2005; Zhang, 2006). Especially important is focusing on the whole message and on the overall context of the communication (Gass and Varonis 1984), i.e. listening for meaning rather than attending to individual sounds. If you get stuck, some of the literature suggests asking the customer to write down their request (Kumar and Suresh, 2000; Osa et al., 2006; de Souza, 1996).

To summarise, some factors that can encourage effective listening include:

- establishing a rapport with the other person;

- making appropriate, regular, eye contact (but be aware of cultural differences);

- smiling;

- using the customer's names where possible/appropriate;

- nodding (but be aware of cultural differences);

- having an appropriate, accepting facial expression;

- leaning towards the customer (but don't invade personal space);
- sitting adjacent to – or at an angle to – the customer rather than opposite them;
- concentrating on what the customer is saying;
- showing an interest in what is being said;
- assessing *what* is being said not *how* it is being said;
- using open questions;
- pausing to allow the customer to speak;
- listening for ideas and concepts;
- not jumping to conclusions or looking for quick-fixes;
- being open-minded;
- keeping emotions in check;
- being aware of your own biases and prejudices;
- checking understanding;
- using verbal prompts (e.g. 'can you tell me more?');
- asking probing and open-ended questions to clarify meaning (e.g. 'how did you feel about that?');
- using playback (e.g. repeating a key word without breaking the customer's train of thought);
- paraphrasing what the customer has said to further discussion without interrupting their thoughts;
- not interrupting;
- avoiding distractions.

Case study: 'I don't hear what you say...'

An undergraduate studying for a degree in information management and library studies was due to be sent on a four-week work-experience placement. Arrangements were made for him to go to a prestigious local museum, which had a significant research library. He was carefully briefed before his departure, and was allocated a personal mentor from the university library staff. The mentor explained that the student should look on this not just as work experience, but also as an opportunity to add to his CV, and to perhaps even obtain a potential reference. The mentor arranged for the student to check in with them weekly via telephone, to provide a short update on how the placement was proceeding.

When the student arrived at the museum, he was pleasantly surprised to find that a genuine effort had been made to provide him with a 'real project', and that he would not merely be passed around departments to gain general, if rather superficial experience. His project, which was to last the entire four weeks of his placement, would be to produce a new 'general guide to using museum facilities'. This was to take the form of a pamphlet, which would also be available online, and which would make use of existing media (illustrations, notes etc.) from the various departments of the museum.

The student eagerly started the project, and for whatever reason, perhaps because he was a mature student who the museum management did not feel the need to supervise closely, he was largely left to his own devices for the next four weeks. As arranged, he contacted his university mentor on a weekly basis, although this largely consisted of reassuring his mentor that all was well.

When the four weeks was up, the museum management were both surprised and disappointed to discover that what the student had come up with – far from being a pamphlet and online version – was in fact a flow diagram. It was a very carefully considered and technically complex, animated, interactive IT-based flow diagram, in which the student had made full use of his previous experience in computer programming and website design – but it was not what the museum had asked for.

The subsequent debrief, which was attended by the mentor, student and museum management, gave the student a rather poor assessment of his work-placement project. The student subsequently appealed the poor result through the university, but the appeal was rejected.

When the student returned to coursework at his university, he continued to exhibit a marked inability to follow instructions. Even the more practical aspects of his submissions to his course tutors were often wildly over-theorised, and bore no real relationship to what he had actually been asked to do. Despite significant efforts to steer him in the right direction, all attempts failed, and the student was eventually asked to leave.

Lessons learned

- If you are monitoring a student on a work placement, ensure that there are measurables with which you can accurately check progress. Basic 'howgozits' will only elicit a general 'OK thanks' response.

- Ensure that the student clearly understands what the work placement manager requires in terms of actual deliverables, and that there will be regular, local progress checks.

- Be prepared to accept that, despite your best intentions and all the close assistance in the world, there will still be the occasional (fortunately very rare) student who just cannot take instructions, and is hence not capable of absorbing a university education. However hard it seems, once you have recognised this, it is time to say 'goodbye'.

Exemplar: Secret shoppers at Monroe County Public Library, Indiana

Use of a secret shopper or mystery shopper/consumer involves sending out field researchers posing as shoppers to carry out real transactions in a retail or service setting. Alternatively, they may instead be required to make phone-calls to the retail outlets or services. Whichever method is used, they are likely to have a list of questions to ask or a series of interactions to initiate in order to test response times, answers to questions etc.

In 2005, Monroe County Public Library (MCPL) partnered with secret shopping programme specialists from the Indiana Small Business Development Center to develop a programme tailored to the library's needs. Library managers were asked to collaborate by offering suggestions on the aspects of public service that they were most interested in evaluating, and in helping develop realistic scenarios for the shoppers and which the shoppers felt comfortable with. The shoppers chosen matched the demographics of MCPL's patron base, i.e. a cross-section of the local community, including customers with English as a second language, students, people with disabilities, parents with children, etc.

Among the impressions the shoppers were instructed to record were the friendliness and approachability of staff, and the thoroughness of the reference interviews they encountered.

To ensure that individual shopping experiences were generalisable and to control variations, multiple shopping experiences were scheduled for each service point targeted on various days and at various times. To avoid perceptions of secret shopping as 'spying' and resulting in distrust and finger-pointing, references to staff names remained confidential.

Generally, the results showed the staff performed well in terms of friendliness, professionalism and answering questions. One area where they performed less well was approachability, with some shoppers reporting that staff seemed preoccupied or that they did not initiate contact with customers. Multi-tasking and the presence of technology at service points were identified as potential barriers resulting in this perception. As a consequence of this finding, MCPL managers encouraged staff to become more proactive in approaching customers and to be mindful of the workloads they brought to the reference desk. As well as identifying such issues, the programme was used to create positive discussions among staff about customer service, and productive suggestions were subsequently made about such issues as workplace communications and scheduling. The integration of such a programme into the overall customer service environment of the library is vital, as is promotion of the programme in a positive, open manner, so that staff feel involved and empowered in solution seeking.

Unlike surveys and comments forms, a secret shopper programme describes actual experiences rather than reporting perceptions, and therefore affords the library an opportunity to create a deliberate, controlled stream of information about its performance that can be repeated regularly to identify issues before they escalate into complaints.

Writing on the secret shopper initiative, Steve Backs says: 'I wanted to use this project as a way to improve not only individual performance, but also to cause myself and other managers to think about steps we could take to reduce barriers to providing the best possible service' (Backs and Kinder, 2007).

Further reading

Amsberry, D. (2009) 'Using effective listening skills with international patrons', *Reference Services Review* 37(1): 10–19.

Backs, S. M. and Kinder, T. (2007) 'Secret shopping at the Monroe County Public Library', *Indiana Libraries* 26(4): 17–19.

Burkamp, M. and Virbick, D. (2002) 'Through the eyes of a secret shopper', *American Libraries* 33(10): 56–7.

Curry, A. and Copeman, D. (2005) 'Reference service to international students: a field stimulation research study', *Journal of Academic Librarianship* 31(5): 409–20.

De Souza, Y. (1996) 'Reference work with international students: making the most use of the neutral question', *Reference Services Review* 24(4): 41–8.

Derwing, T. M., Rossiter, M. J. and Munro, M. J. (2002) 'Teaching native speakers to listen to foreign-accented speech', *Journal of Multilingual and Multicultural Development* 23(4): 245–59.

Fayer, J. M. and Krasinski, E. (1987) 'Native and non-native judgments of intelligibility and irritation', *Language Learning* 37(3): 313–26.

Gass, S. and Varonis, E. M. (1984) 'The effect of familiarity on the comprehensibility of non-native speech', *Language Learning* 34(1): 65–89.

Kumar, S. L. and Suresh, R. S. (2000) 'Strategies for providing effective reference services for international adult learners', *Reference Librarian* 33(69): 327–36.

Levi, S. V., Winters, S. J. and Pisoni, D. B. (2007) 'Speaker-independent factors affecting the perception of foreign accent in a second language', *Journal of the Acoustical Society of America* 121(4): 2327–38.

Osa, J. O., Nyana, S. A. and Ogbaa, C. A. (2006) 'Effective cross-cultural communication to enhance reference transactions: training guidelines and tips', *Knowledge Quest* 35(2): 22–4.

Sarkodie-Mensah, K. (1992) 'Dealing with international students in a multicultural era', *Journal of Academic Librarianship* 18(2): 214–6.

Van Der Wiele, T., Hesselink, M. and Van Iwaarden, J. (2005) 'Secret shopping: A tool to develop insight into customer service provision', *Total Quality Management* 16(4): 529–41.

Zhang, L. (2006) 'Communication in academic libraries: an East Asian perspective', *Reference Services Review* 34(1): 164–76.

7

Handling complaints

Rather than trying to reduce the number of complaints, organizations need to encourage staff to seek out complaints because this will define what customers want. (J. Barlow and C. Møller)

Just look at companies like Tesco. Canny customer relationship management, targeted marketing and successful customer profiling has ensured that the retailer has become one of the most trusted brands in the UK, with customer loyalty at a premium. For such a huge organisation, covering a massive range of services – from groceries into financial services and new media – they still manage to have a streamlined approach to customer service and the organisation is fully joined-up. When you consider how successfully they do it, it's easy to see why the public gets frustrated with the public sector maze. (P. Bentham)

Aims

The aims of this chapter are as follows:

- to identify the appropriate steps in handling customer complaints;
- to develop a positive proactive response to customers' problems and complaints.

To assist with planning, Table 7.1 presents a suggested session plan.

Table 7.1 Session plan – handling complaints

Session	Aims	Content	Methods	Aids	Time (mins)
Handling complaints	To identify the appropriate steps in handling customer complaints		T		10
		I have a complaint	A	H/O	20
	To develop a more positive proactive response to customers' problems and complaints		T		10
		As a rule...	A	H/O	15
		Scenarios	A	H/O	15
Approx. total time (mins)					70

*A, activity (participants); F/C, flipchart; H/O, handout; P/I, Post-it notes; T, talk (facilitator)

Background

Even if your customer service is excellent, some customers will experience problems and, as a result, will complain. A complaint arises in a situation where:

- we have failed to meet the customer's needs, expectations or requirements; and
- an apology, explanation, resolution and/or possible financial redress are required.

The National Library of Australia defines a complaint as 'a formal expression of dissatisfaction received in writing, or through follow-up in person/by phone by dissatisfied user with supervisor or other senior staff (that is where extra effort is made to complain)' (Missingham, 2001: 151).

Failure to meet the customer's needs, expectations or requirements may be because those expectations exceed what you are able to offer, or because your service's procedures have not been followed. Sometimes, the customer will raise the complaint and, on occasion, you may anticipate a complaint because you are aware of a problem before the customer is. Either way, you need to address the issue to stop it happening again.

Not all customers give us helpful cues such as 'I want to complain about...' or 'I am annoyed that...', so be aware that neither a query or simple request for information, nor a request for clarification of action taken, necessarily constitute complaints.

If in doubt, ask the customer whether or not they wish to lodge a complaint. In many cases, dissatisfied customers simply want to have their say rather than lodge an official complaint. Generally, such customers become angry or abusive only when they feel they are getting nowhere. The next chapter will cover dealing with such customers. Ideally, most issues can be resolved before they escalate.

The previous chapters have discussed how to prevent matters escalating to either a formal complaint or a confrontational situation. One of the main recommendations is to listen actively to what your customer has to say, paying close attention to what is said, without interrupting, and noting the key points. Not all customers complain on the spot. The ways they choose to complain are reflective of different genders (Gruber et al., 2009), cultures and personalities. Some may leave your service area, mull things over and then e-mail or phone to complain. Your other communication skills should come into practice in such instances.

Complaints are usually about processes, procedures or systems, so don't take them personally. Accept that things go wrong from time to time. What counts is how well and how quickly you sort things out. Lord offers the following mantra:

> This person isn't a problem,
> This person has a problem.
> I'm not the problem.
> I'm the person who might be able to help address this person's problem.

(Lord, 2003: 18)

Lord goes on to say that depersonalising an encounter in this way helps staff to follow the next 'and perhaps most important commandment' – listen – as we highlighted in the previous chapter.

As a representative of your organisation, in the customer's eyes, you *are* the organisation. When you listen to the customer's complaint, you take responsibility for solving the problem. How you deal with the problem-solving will leave a lasting image of the organisation with the customer.

According to the proverb, 'a good reputation arrives on foot, and leaves on horseback'. We used to say that customers receiving good service would, on average, tell 11 other people about it. By contrast, customers receiving poor service would, on average, tell 20 other people. Nowadays, of course, we live in the so-called global village, and media reports of poor service circulate worldwide.

One of the best pieces of advice is to put yourself in the customer's shoes and maintain a positive attitude. First, as we have said, listen to the customer. This gives them a chance to let off steam and gives you a chance to pick up clues about what really matters to them.

By listening carefully and by picking up on body language and general demeanour, you can assess the mood of your customer – are they frustrated, inconvenienced, annoyed? When you apologise on behalf of your organisation, choose words that accurately reflect this mood, e.g. 'I understand why you are feeling ... frustrated/inconvenienced/annoyed' and so forth.

Do not try to turn the tables on them and blame them in some way. Do not blame other sections of the organisation. Do not become defensive, try to make excuses, or argue. Just focus on the fact that the customer is not satisfied. From the outset, you should believe that 'the customer is always right' and be open-minded about their opinion. Of course, complaints are sometimes unjustified and the customer may well be wrong. If this is one of those times, you need to manage the complaint in such a way that they can leave with dignity and without being overly embarrassed.

Recall Chapter 5, and use positive words rather than negatives in your interaction with the customer. Use open questions to determine the customer's expectations/suggestions so that you can work towards resolving the issue in a way that satisfies the customer and does not compromise your organisation. This can be done by explaining first what you can do and then gently adding what you cannot do. Between you, the options can then be discussed and the best fit decided upon.

Any action that is agreed should be acted upon promptly in the time promised, and the customer should be updated on progress and resolution.

Bear in mind that customer complaints are a form of customer feedback. Sometimes a customer complaint affords us an opportunity to impress a customer in a way that would not have been possible had everything gone smoothly. Feedback in the form of customer complaints affords the organisation opportunities to improve its procedures, processes and systems. It can highlight recurrent issues or draw attention to falling standards and, by so doing, lead to further development of your customer care culture. Thus, while you may not feel like it at the time, it is a good idea to thank your customer for making the complaint because it has given you a chance to improve your service in future.

After dealing with a complaint, you might like to reflect on the lessons you have learned from the encounter and what else you might do on the basis of the experience, e.g. production of an explanatory/informational leaflet covering the points raised, or construction of a questionnaire or survey to ascertain customers' perceptions of the aspect of the service which led to the complaint. You might also consider whether or not there is any more you can do for the customer who raised the complaint, e.g. phoning to check that they were satisfied with the outcome, or sending them a letter of appreciation. Taking the initiative can make all the difference between adequate customer service and excellent customer service. Initiative does not mean stepping outside of the organisational rules/regulations – it means giving value-added in whatever way you can.

Figure 7.1 presents a scale of attitudes to complaints, ranging from negative to positive.

Your organisation may keep a customer comments/complaints book and may also log complaints received. If it does not, do you think it should? To reiterate, when a complaint is received, it highlights problem areas or recurring issues and affords an opportunity to look for (and identify) the root of the problem. The customer perceives only the symptoms of the problem. You may need to investigate further to get to the cause. The information generated – identifying what needs to be done, by whom, who needs to know and by when – then enables you to improve future customer service. If policies or procedures need to be adapted, the 'by whom' will be someone with the appropriate authority and influence. This person should be striving for continuous improvement by exploring patterns and trends in respect of complaints; however, we can all play our part. Chapter 10 on suggestions for improvement gives participants a chance to make their own contributions.

An organisation that responds to customer complaints proactively and views complaints as part of a learning process will have a better public image and will also gain respect from the customer.

Figure 7.1   Negative and positive attitudes to complaints

NEGATIVE	Ignored	Patronised	Reacted to	Responded to	Encouraged	POSITIVE
	Denied	Defended	Listened to	Understood	Welcomed	

Aim 1: To identify the appropriate steps in handling customer complaints

The four 'd's of behaviour

Complaints come in many forms, and are delivered in many different styles. The following four categories represent 'broad brush' groupings to cover the many shades of behaviour that the complainant may exhibit. For each one of the four categories, a suggested style of response is offered, which may assist in achieving that happy state of mutual satisfaction which should be the aim of any attempt to resolve a complaint.

- *Distant* – shy, silent, doesn't like to complain/comment:
  - give strong positive reinforcement when they do comment;
  - may prefer to complain in writing rather than face to face.
- *Defies* – belligerent, gripes:
  - acknowledge positive contribution and valid points;
  - reinforce idea of solving issues together.
- *Dominates* – over-talkative, caught up in their own agenda:
  - try to impose time limit;
  - may need to offer individual attention away from public gaze (audience).
- *Distracts* – goes off topic:
  - refocus attention – state the relevant point;
  - ask how opinion relates to issue under discussion.

Steps for handling complaints

The procedure for handling complaints can be broken into eight basic steps:

1. Say 'thank you'.
2. Explain why you appreciate the complaint.
3. Apologise for the mistake.
4. Promise to do something about it.
5. Ask for the necessary information.
6. Correct the mistake – promptly.
7. Check customer satisfaction.
8. Prevent further mistakes.

Formal complaints procedures

Your institution will no doubt have its own formal complaints procedure. In this increasingly litigious age, such procedures are an essential part of the fabric of our working lives. All staff should therefore be fully familiar with such procedures, and should be able to offer informed guidance to any customer wishing to make a formal complaint.

Below, we have created a generic procedure for a fictional university library. This can be used as a basis for discussion – participants may wish to compare it with the procedure at their own institution.

Plateglass Library and Information Services compliments and complaints procedure

Purpose

The purpose of this procedure is to enable customer compliments and complaints to be dealt with effectively and to take corrective action where necessary.

Procedure

- All compliments and complaints should be noted on the form below and passed to the customer services manager.
- The customer services manager will acknowledge a complaint within X working days of receipt of the complaint.
- The complaint will be investigated and any necessary corrective action will be implemented. The complainant will be notified of the library's response and any action taken within X weeks of the complaint being received.
- Copies of all correspondence relating to the complaint or compliment will be forwarded to the organisation's records and information manager for retention.
- All compliments and complaints will be recorded and an annual report produced.

Plateglass Library and Information Services compliments and complaints form

We would like to know what you think about the service that you have received. Feedback is important to us, as we can use it to improve our services.

We hope that you find our service efficient, friendly and competent. If you would like to write to us about it, please do so on this form and send it to the Customer Services Manager, Plateglass Library and Information Services, Plateglass University, Foresight Road, Hopeville, RU1 1AM or send an e-mail to: *csm@plais.edu.uk*

Name:

Address for reply:

Comments:

Date:

I have a complaint...

For this activity, the participants are divided into two or three groups, each of which is given a copy of a table with four headings: Situation, Procedure, Exceptions and Recovery. 'Situation' involves the focus of the complaint; 'Procedure' involves the custom and practice for dealing with such a complaint; 'Exception' refers to any factors which alter the procedure; 'Recovery' is how the complaint should be or is handled.

Using real-life complaints from the organisation's complaints book/log or from the examples given below, participants are then asked to complete the grid as appropriate. The following examples are based on real-life customers' comments, some or all of which may be identified as complaints:

- 'I'm fed up with not being able to find issues of the *Journal of Civil Engineering*. My tutor steered me towards Issue 3/09 as there is an article in it by a colleague of his which he thinks would be particularly helpful in my current assignment. I did find the journal last week, and had a quick skim through it. I've come back today to spend the afternoon working on it, and it's nowhere to be found. Not only that, but another issue with a related article has also gone walkabout. I thought that people weren't allowed to take journals out of the library. I'm really stuck now, as my assignment is due in next week, and I can't get the article I need to complete it.'

- 'I'm studying sports science and it seems to me that you have a fairly limited book stock in this area – certainly compared with tourism – which seems to have loads. Quite often you don't seem to have the books that my tutor puts on the suggested further reading list – and even when you are supposed to have stock it's usually only one or two, and they're always out – not surprising when there's 47 people on my course.'

- 'I know you've got a "silent floor" in the library, but it's so popular I can hardly ever get a seat in there. As for the so-called "quiet discussion permitted" areas on the other floors, they're anything but quiet, and I find the noise level unacceptable. Sometimes it's like a common room in there. This is a library. Why can't it be "silence please" everywhere?'

- 'Because of the way my lectures are programmed I usually end up coming to the library at lunchtime to get books. Every time I come here there's always a massive queue at the library counter, and it annoys me to see three or four library staff who could be "queue busters" just sitting at their desks with a sandwich or whatever. I've got a part-time job at Tesco and they just won't let queues build up – ever. It's "all hands to the pumps", and people get served quickly. Why can't it be like that here?'

- 'Your computerised stock control system here just isn't up to it. I very often find that although the OPAC is telling me that something is "not on loan", when I go to the correct shelf location it's just not there. It's not just me, either. Quite a few of my friends are having the same problem, and it's very frustrating. Why is this happening to us?'

- 'I've just turned one of the computers on the third floor and there's a disgusting pornographic screensaver on it. There are some real sickos around if that's how they have to get their kicks. A female overseas student was sat next to me when I turned it on. She saw it and immediately picked up her books and left. I hope she doesn't think it had anything to do with me. I found it very embarrassing. Is there any way you can trace who might have done it? They need to be stopped.'

- 'I've just been up to the first floor and yet again, the photocopying machine has broken down. It's bad enough that we have to pay to use it, and I wouldn't mind so much if it was reliable, but it's not. I'm seriously considering buying myself a cheap printer with copying facility so I can do it myself.'

- 'I'm under a lot of pressure at the moment to finish an assignment, and my laptop is in for repair, so I have to use the library's PCs. When I came in today I found that the area I'd intended working in, plus its six PCs, has been taken over for some sort of library workshop. Nobody told me about this, and it doesn't seem to have been advertised that well. Certainly none of my friends knew about it either. I'm stuck now. Is there anything you can do to help?'

- 'I lost my library card three days ago, and it's caused me a lot of stress. I don't mind paying £5 for a new one – it's the thought that someone might have found my card and may be using it to steal books. A friend of mine at Boxton University had this happen to him, and ended up being charged over £200 for books someone had stolen in his name. There was nothing he could do about it. Not only that, but when I checked this morning at the library helpdesk, my card was in lost property and had been there since yesterday – but no one told me. Just a quick phone call to me could have saved me from a lot of worry.'

Sample responses to the above customer feedback are given in Table 7.2.

Table 7.2   Sample responses to customer feedback

Situation	Procedure	Exceptions	Recovery
Customer reports a missing issue of a journal	Check shelves, journal receipts and binding list Complete 'missing' slip	Is electronic version available? Is interlibrary loan available? Is item available in a nearby library?	Speedier shelving of journals Photocopies of missing issues Binding done sooner Stock checks made more regularly
Student customer believes book stock in subject area is inadequate	Book ordering is down to the schools not the library Refer to lecturer/school/tutor Student can complete a book suggestion slip	Is interlibrary loan available if student has specific missing title in mind	Student book suggestion slips Nominated direct contact within school to refer to such issues
Customer says that counter is understaffed during lunch periods	Maintain a minimum number of staff (3)	Query handling may impact, as may course attendance and sickness	Stagger lunch periods Have reserve list of staff to cover/call upon Introduce more self-service points Train shelving staff for emergency desk cover

Table 7.2   Sample responses to customer feedback (*Cont'd*)

Situation	Procedure	Exceptions	Recovery
			Consider introducing a 'queuebuster' response as per many supermarkets and train staff to provide emergency cover
Customer cannot find book on shelf although the online catalogue says it is 'not on loan'	Check shelves, trolleys awaiting shelving, items under repair etc. Change status of book to 'missing/lost'	Check adequacy, clarity of signage/guidance 'Not on loan' does not equate with 'on the shelf'	Buy or borrow a replacement book
Customer complains about a pornographic screensaver, loaded by a 'hacker' onto a PC	Offending screen to be covered immediately Technical staff to remove screensaver, check firewalls etc.	Might the complainant be the hacker, testing the system? It may be worth recording names of those reporting incidents	Offer customer complimentary time on a PC away from the offensive one. Apologise for any embarrassment caused and say checks will be made to try to identify the culprit (e.g. CCTV)
Customer complains that the photocopying machine on one floor is frequently out of order	Checks to be made by library staff in first instance Maintenance staff to be called Out-of-order sign to be put on machine	Out-of-order sign to contain information about locations of other photocopiers	Frequency of breakdown to be logged Terms of contract and call-out time to be reviewed and discussed with maintenance company

Table 7.2 Sample responses to customer feedback (*Cont'd*)

Situation	Procedure	Exceptions	Recovery
Customer complains about noise levels in 'quiet discussion' area	There is a 'total silence area' – but is it large enough for the potential customer population? Stewards/shelvers to 'police' floors to maintain silence and 'quiet' discussion Tannoy announcements can be made CCTV covers floor areas but gives only 'snapshots' as staff cannot be constantly monitoring the screens	Is the customer overly sensitive to levels or is there really an issue? Different customer perceptions of acceptable noise levels in 'quiet discussion'	Ensure stewards/shelvers know that maintenance of both silence and 'quiet' discussion is part of their remit They also need to know what backup is available when they are having difficulty maintaining silence Have a definition of, e.g. 'quiet discussion', so that staff are confident to step in when noise levels are rising Are notices clear enough, intelligible to diverse user population? Possible usage of seminar room by customer Ensure that the 'silent study' area is large enough for the number of potential users
Student complains that she came to use a library PC and found that the area in which she intended working had been taken over by a library workshop	Direct student to the nearest free PC in the library or book her the next available slot Offer a loanable laptop if one is available	Library workshop may have been well advertised in advance but student left coming in until the last minute	Post a sign giving locations, hours of opening and types of computers, software etc. of all facilities on campus Maybe 24-hour opening labs, e.g. in science and maths blocks

Table 7.2　Sample responses to customer feedback *(Cont'd)*

Situation	Procedure	Exceptions	Recovery
Member of the library complains that he lost his card and, although it was handed in to the library desk, he was not notified as to its whereabouts, causing him stress	Library cards left on the premises are generally put in 'lost and found' but, time permitting, staff will contact readers to notify them Ensure a 'stop' is put on a library card as soon as it is reported lost	Cards can get buried among other lost property in 'lost and found' Staff may be too busy to find time to call	Separate area for library cards Evening staff charged with going through these in off-peak times to ensure notification within 24 hours Reassure the customer that a 'stop' is put on any card as soon as it is reported lost

Garvey (2008) describes other scenarios – not necessarily complaint-based, and resolutions particularly aimed at law library staff but relevant in other sectors also.

An alternative way to analyse customer service situations is to use a chart with the following headings:

- analysis;
- scale of problem;
- present situation;
- desired situation;
- action needed.

Having such a chart can help staff to gather facts, identify difficulties involved and move on from the complaint to the actions that need to be taken to resolve it. Documents such as these two examples may also be used as contributions to an organisation's risk register as they help to identify weaknesses in the service which are potential risks to organisational reputation. Analysing them in this way gives some indication of how best to rectify the situation and minimise the risk in the future.

Aim 2: To develop a positive proactive response to customers' problems and complaints

Can we compare libraries with the retail sector?

In 2009, Channel 4 screened a television series entitled *I'm Running Sainsbury's*. One particular episode featured a customer service manager, Niall, from the Enfield branch of the supermarket chain. He was in charge of a 'Here to Help' desk for issues/complaints in store. The main role of the desk was to issue refunds/exchanges. Niall was of the opinion that some customers could not be bothered to queue there to complain, so left dissatisfied. He therefore proposed the opening of a 'customer surgery' to listen to, and fix, complaints in-store and straight away. His idea was trialled at the store's Finchley Road branch in East London. Over a ten-day period, the surgery received 256 visitors, 84 per cent of which said they would not have aired their problem had the surgery not been there. In total, 142 customers (55 per cent) had their problems solved immediately. Having exceeded his customer satisfaction target of 50 per cent, Niall's idea was rolled out and Niall was seconded to the customer service division at head office.

In conjunction with the surgeries, Niall and his colleagues installed a whiteboard in the foyer with a heading 'All said and done', with illustrations of customer comments in black speech bubbles and the company responses in red speech bubbles – an idea that might be adopted by libraries.

One of the issues that emerged during the supermarket customer surgeries was the impersonal nature of self-service checkout, and how customers like to speak to a person. To ensure that speed was coupled with the personal touch, the number of 'baskets only' or 'ten items or less' tills was increased. With so many self-service points in libraries, is this something from which we can learn? Robertson and Shaw (2005) comment that when self-service technology (SST) fails to perform as promised, customers don't always have the reassurance of service staff to assist them, nor do service staff have the opportunity to prompt customers to voice their dissatisfaction. SST may rely on customers to initiate their own complaint response; should customers fail to do so, the organisation may not know that a problem exists. How can organisations with SST-based facilities encourage customers to complain directly to the organisation?

There is much in the literature about the viability of comparing the service sectors such as libraries with the retail sector (Van Fleet and Wallace, 2002; Horner, 2005; Brannon, 2006; McCabe et al., 2007; Rudd, 2007; Siess, 2007; Bernstein, 2008; Paterson, 2008). It is not a new comparison: Van Fleet and Wallace quote Samuel Swett Green:

> A librarian should be as unwilling to allow an inquirer to leave the library with his question unanswered as a shopkeeper to have a customer go out of his store without a purchase. Receive investigators with something of the cordiality displayed by an old-time shopkeeper. Hold on to them until they have obtained the information they are seeking, and show a persistency in supplying their wants similar to that manifested by a successful clerk in effecting a sale. (Green, 1876: 79)

Rudd (2007) asks, 'if you compared your library to a customer service model like Nordstrom, how would it size up?', adding, 'your library's success may very well depend on the answer to that question' (Rudd, 2007: 142). If you are not familiar with Nordstrom, the article by Bernstein (2008) outlines and comments the firm's service principles – product knowledge, courtesy, solution-oriented, follow-through, coordination and professionalism.

Incidentally, three of the best library assistants with whom we have worked came from different sectors: one had been a flight attendant, one a dental nurse and one an assistant in the children's shoe concession of a large department store.

As a rule...

Depending on their organisation, facilitators may like to have a quiz about the rules/regulations/procedures underpinning their customer service. This helps to determine the participants' awareness of the procedures to be followed when dealing with complaints.

Given the diversity of regulations in different organisations, it is difficult to produce an all-encompassing questionnaire, but the following may give you some ideas:

- Who is entitled to use the library service for reference purposes?
- Who is entitled to borrow material from the library?
- What is the normal loan period for books?

- What identification do people need to be able to use the service/borrow material?
- How many times may material be reissued to the same borrower?
- When may an item not be reissued to a borrower?
- If fines are charged, what are the rates?
- Can persons causing a nuisance be asked to leave the library? If so, under what circumstances may they be readmitted?
- If a serious breach of library regulations occurs, may the infringer be suspended? If so, for how long?
- What is the maximum number of books that may be taken out at any one time?

As Gardner (2005) points out, customer complaints may in fact alert you to regulations and policies that need to change. Some longstanding regulations/policies may hold less validity currently. Gardner gives examples of customer service situations in which adherence to regulations/policies has lost customers or at least their goodwill, and suggests cases where exceptions could have been made. Huebert and Nixon (2004) similarly debate bureaucracy in public libraries and the potential implications of strict implementation on customer service. Talley and Axelroth (2001) suggest looking at each and every policy and procedure from the customer's viewpoint, pointing out that certain regulations/policies are devised for the benefit of library staff rather than customers.

Scenarios

The following scenarios are suggested as starting points for discussion regarding the issues raised in this session. There is no 'preferred solution', although in any such situation there are certainly things you should or should not do.

Do:

- thank the complainant for bringing the matter to your attention;
- obtain full details of the complaint, and the surrounding circumstances;
- use open questions to determine the customer's expectations/ suggestions so that you can work towards resolving the issue in a way that satisfies the customer and does not compromise your organisation;

- if no immediate solution is available, say that you will investigate promptly, and will contact the complainant with feedback within 24 hours;

- obtain corroborating information/evidence relating to the complaint;

- if you are subjected to personal abuse or to discrimination, stand your ground in a cool, calm and collected manner, and make it clear that this is unacceptable to you personally and to the institution;

- carefully explain any rules or regulations that are pertinent to the situation, always remembering that a degree of flexibility may be good for customer relations – but only if appropriate;

- ensure that you provide the promised feedback to the complainant within the appropriate timescale.

Don't:

- be provoked;

- try to pass the buck, whether onto 'the system', or another department;

- make promises you either can't or won't keep;

- provide 'knee-jerk' responses – they are usually way off mark;

- be negative in your manner.

A clash of cultures

You are a young woman administrator in the accommodation office of an organisation that leases houses from private landlords and lets them to students. The management is entirely your responsibility and landlords are guaranteed a rent and freedom from landlord–tenant disputes.

A male postgraduate student, a senior civil servant from a foreign country, has been living with his wife and children in one of the properties you manage. They are moving out and, as is normal, the house has been inspected by one of your staff with a view to determining whether the student's deposit (required against possible damage) can be refunded. Your assistant reports that there is damage, especially in the kitchen area, and that essential repairs and redecoration will exceed the amount of the deposit, which has to be withheld. She has not seen the student himself as he was out, but his wife has been told they are to lose their deposit.

The student comes to see you, brushes aside your assistant's verdict and demands that the deposit be refunded. It is clear he has told his wife that he will put matters right and sort things out, as the head of the household. You hold your ground and refuse the refund. He then demands to see the owner of the house (whom he knows to be a man of his own age). In line with the agreement you have with the landlords, you refuse politely and tell him he has to deal with you.

At this he explodes, bangs the table and shouts, 'You are a woman! You are my junior! You do not give me orders!'

Do you...

- let the matter drop and make a refund 'just this once';
- hold your ground and calmly and politely tell him of western principles of sex equality;
- find a large male cleaner to repeat your decision to him;
- or something else?

You are the registrar to whom the young woman accommodation officer reports. The day after the above incident, the international officer from the students' union comes to see you to say that she has had a complaint from the foreign postgraduate that, during the altercation on the previous day, your accommodation officer was racially abusive to him, saying, 'can't you understand plain English?'

She is demanding that the accommodation officer be disciplined and the deposit refunded. If you refuse she intends to take the matter to the principal.

The international officer has a reputation for tenacity and winning cases she takes up.

Last week, the principal told you he hopes to be invited to the student's country during the next academic year to give a series of lectures at the university from which the postgraduate student received his first degree.

Do you...

- agree to refund the deposit, provided the complaint is withdrawn;
- make the accommodation officer apologise;
- stand your ground over the complaint and insist that the international officer view the state of the kitchen;
- keep your head down and refer the dispute to the principal;
- or something else?

I thought you were my friend...

The following scenario questions are suitable for student workers or more junior staff:

- A roommate or a student comes into the library to take out a book but has forgotten their ID. The person says, 'But you know me, just let me take out the book'. What would you do?

- A student or a roommate comes into the library to take out book and their account shows 'delinquent', meaning that their account is overdue. The person promises to bring back the book tomorrow, the next day at the latest, if you let them take out the book now. What would you do?

- One of your friends comes up to the desk when you are working and wants to talk about non-work issues for a long time. What would you do?

Case studies

Revenge is a dish best served with musical accompaniment

Airlines are notoriously stingy when they are called upon to compensate passengers for lost or damaged luggage – particularly where the item or items concerned are of high value. When Dave Carroll, a Canadian musician, recently travelled with a major North American airline, he entrusted his precious Taylor acoustic guitar to their tender care. Imagine his horror when fellow passengers started shouting that the baggage handlers were throwing guitars around. And yes, on arrival at his destination, the Taylor was in pieces.

After unsuccessfully attempting to obtain full compensation from the airline in question over a year-long period, a very frustrated Dave Carroll then composed the song, 'United breaks guitars', and posted it on YouTube. With 4 million views in the first ten days, not only was his offering a massive internet hit, but its wider impact was such that shares in the airline lost 10 per cent of their value (approx. $180m). Dave's satirical video, which cost a mere £90 to make, brought him international recognition, with appearances on breakfast television in both the USA and the UK. Not surprisingly, after the runaway success of the video, the airline then offered Dave some £700 in compensation, plus some flight vouchers. (Note, however, that the repair costs alone would have been approximately £1,000). At this stage, however, Dave told the airline that he would rather they donated the money to charity.

This saga does however have a happy ending: Taylor has most generously provided Dave with a free replacement guitar (great customer service and marketing!), and more significantly for our purposes, the airline has decided to use the video for training purposes, in order to highlight what can happen if you ignore customer service – in this case an astronomically expensive $180m lesson in reduced share price (the equivalent of three Boeing 737s at 2009 prices).

Lessons learned

- If you mess up big-style, don't prevaricate. Accept responsibility and respond promptly and positively to your seriously dissatisfied customer in order to rectify the situation.

- Don't imagine that your dissatisfied customer can only cause you limited damage. The days when you only told your next-door neighbour that the village butcher was using too much bread in his sausages are long gone. The advent of the internet and of social networking sites in particular means that in terms of communicative power, we are certainly in a 'global village'. One broken guitar, one song on YouTube – 4 million hits in ten days, and massive damage to the company share price. The power of the individual consumer has never been as strong as it is today.

- If you do offer compensation, make sure that your customer is not left feeling that they have been fobbed off, or that they have been short-changed. Do that and you are compounding the felony, and will simply create even more negative publicity.

- At the very least, if you do experience such a disaster in terms of customer service, make very sure that you learn from it, and that it does not happen again. The airline in question has recognised this and is now using the video for its own staff training programme.

The jobsworth

A pilot went to the equipment store to obtain a replacement item for his faulty aircrew watch. On checking stock, the storeman advised him that he couldn't let him have one immediately as there was only one left. An order had already been placed for additional stock, which was forecast for delivery within the next week. When the pilot asked why he couldn't have the one remaining item, he was advised that 'quantity 1' was the 'minimum establishment level', below which the stock level could not be allowed to fall. The pilot asked to speak to the sergeant in charge of the store, who resolved the situation and issued the watch. The sergeant also corrected the store man's interpretation of the regulations, and explained to him that the 'minimum establishment' figure of 'quantity 1' was simply a device to automatically trigger resupply, and should not be interpreted as 'always keep one in stock'.

Analysis

The storeman genuinely believed that he was interpreting the regulations correctly, and lost sight of the primary task of providing good customer care. You will no doubt be able to think of many situations in your own life where the 'rules and regulations' have got in the way of providing you with good service. At its worst, this produces the stereotypical 'jobsworth' approach, in which the person who is supposed to be providing you with a service appears more interested in interpreting the rules to suit his/her own desire to actually deliver as little as possible. This can be as simple as: 'Sorry, my shift ends now' – particularly frustrating for your customer if they are left in limbo because there is no one taking over from you. Don't expect them to be impressed by your 'customer care' as they have the door slammed in their face. There are ways of minimising this particular problem. Supermarkets, for example, typically start to broadcast closure warning messages 15 minute before closing, and count down each five minutes. Communication is all in this context.

How many times have you heard about or even been a frustrated air traveller waiting fruitlessly at an airport to hear any progress with your delayed flight? The best operators realise that even if the flight continues to be delayed, frustration levels can be much reduced simply by keeping passengers advised as to what is actually happening.

So, put processes in place to facilitate good customer care; make sure that your staff both understand and can deliver them; and then communicate with your customers until it hurts.

Just for fun

As we mentioned early on in this chapter, the customer's complaint is not always reasonable. Consider some of the following customer complaints received by Thomas Cook and ABTA in 2003 (with thanks to Alison Wallace of Thomas Cook).

'I think it should be explained in the brochure that the local store does not sell proper biscuits like custard creams or ginger nuts.'

'It's lazy of the local shopkeepers to close in the afternoons. I often needed to buy things during "siesta" time – this should be banned.'

'On my holiday to Goa in India, I was disgusted to find that almost every restaurant served curry. I don't like spicy food at all.'

'We booked an excursion to a water park but no one told us we had to bring our swimming costumes and towels.'

A woman threatened to call police after claiming that she'd been locked in by staff. In fact, she had mistaken the 'do not disturb' sign on the back of the door as a warning to remain in the room.

'We found the sand was not like the sand in the brochure. Your brochure shows the sand as yellow but it was white.'

'We bought "Ray-Ban" sunglasses for five euros (£3.50) from a street trader, only to find out they were fake.'

'No-one told us there would be fish in the sea. The children were startled.'

'It took us nine hours to fly home from Jamaica to England but it only took the Americans three hours to get home.'

'I compared the size of our one-bedroom apartment to our friends' three-bedroom apartment and ours was significantly smaller.'

'There are too many Spanish people. The receptionist speaks Spanish. The food is Spanish. Too many foreigners.'

'We had to queue outside with no air conditioning.'

'It is your duty as a tour operator to advise us of noisy or unruly guests before we travel.'

'I was bitten by a mosquito – no one said they could bite.'

Further reading

Barlow, J. and Møller, C. (2008) *A Complaint is a Gift* (2nd edn), San Francisco, CA: Berrett-Koehler.

Bentham, P. (2007) 'The Varney report: an ideal or a blueprint? The public sector is ready for a services mindshift but only with outside help', available at: *http://www.silicon.com/publicsector/0,3800010403,39167218,00.htm* (accessed 1 October 2009).

Bernstein, M. P. (2008) 'Am I obsolete? How customer service principles ensure the library's relevance', *AALL Spectrum* 13(2): 21–2.

Brannon, S. (2006) 'How working in retail made me a better librarian', One-Person Library 23(2): 6–8.

Gardner, C. A. (2005) 'The importance of customer service', Virginia Libraries 51(4): 2–4.

Garvey, P. A. (2008). 'A walk in the stacks: real-life scenarios and how to deliver good customer service in them', AALL Spectrum 12(8): 20–31.

Green, S. S. (1876) 'Personal relations between librarians and readers', Library Journal 1(2/3): 74–81.

Gruber, T., Szmigin, I. and Voss, R. (2009) 'Handling customer complaints effectively: a comparison of the value maps of female and male complainants', Managing Service Quality 19(6): 636–56.

Horner, D. (2005) 'So much for service', Bookseller, No. 5185, 7 January, 24.

Huebert, J. and Nixon, M (2004) 'Rules, bureaucracy and customer service: a dialogue between two public librarians', PNLA Quarterly 68(3): 10–11.

Lord, C. (2003) 'An access challenge is a customer service opportunity', Alki: the Washington Library Association Journal 19(2): 18–21.

McCabe, D .B., Rosenbaum, M. S. and Yurchsin, J. (2007) 'Perceived service quality and shopping motivations: a dynamic relationship', Services Marketing Quarterly 29(1): 1–21.

McGuigan, G. S. (2002) 'The common sense of customer service: employing advice from the trade and popular literature of business to interactions with irate patrons in libraries', Reference Librarian 36(75/76): 197–204.

Missingham, R. (2001) 'Customer services in the National Library of Australia: leading edge or dragging the chain?' Australian Library Journal 50(2): 147–55.

Nel, D., Athron, T., Pitt, L. F. and Ewing, M. T. (2000) 'Customer evaluations of service complaint experiences in the public sector', Journal of Nonprofit and Public Sector Marketing 7(3): 3–30.

Paterson, N. (2008) 'Are they being served?' Information Scotland 6(1): 17.

Robertson, N. and Shaw, R. (2005) 'Conceptualizing the influence of the self-service technology context on consumer voice', Services Marketing Quarterly 27(2): 33–50.

Siess, J. (2007) 'Lessons from the Nordstrom way: how companies are emulating the #1 customer service company', One-Person Library 23(10): 8–9.

Siess, J. (2006) 'Thinking about …it's all about the customer', One-Person Library 23(2): 1–2.

Talley, M. and Axelroth, J. (2001) 'Talking about customer service', Information Outlook 5(12): 7–10.

Van Fleet, C. and Wallace, D. P. (2002) 'Mr Green's axiom: customer service or just plain good service?' Reference & User Services Quarterly 42(1): 6, 8.

Varney, D. (2006) 'Service transformation: a better service for citizens and businesses, a better deal for the taxpayer', available at: http://www.hm-treasury.gov.uk/d/pbr06_varney_review.pdf (accessed 1 October 2009).

8

Dealing with challenging situations

The pessimist sees the difficulty in very opportunity; the optimist sees the opportunity in every difficulty. (L. P. Jacks)

Smooth seas do not make skilful sailors. (African proverb)

Aims

The aims of this chapter are as follows:

- to identify behaviours that create positive relationships with customers;
- to recognise signs of aggression in a person;
- to identify appropriate strategies for dealing with challenging situations.

To assist with planning, Table 8.1 presents a suggested session plan.

Background

The previous chapter mentioned how dissatisfied customers tell other people about the poor service they receive. It is also worth remembering that for every complaint you hear, there are about 25 others that you don't hear about. Customers who were initially unhappy will only continue using your service and telling other people about its positive aspects if they feel that you have managed to solve their problems. Even angry customers can become more cooperative if you know how to handle them with skill and care. The previous chapters on communication, questioning and active listening should have given you some pointers to this. If the communications material has whetted your appetite, you may also be interested in exploring the concept of 'verbal

Table 8.1 Session plan – dealing with challenging situations

Session	Aims	Content	Methods	Aids	Time (mins)
Dealing with challenging situations	To identify behaviours that create positive relationships with customers		T		10
		Difficult customer consequences	A	H/O	15
	To recognise signs of aggression in a person	Signs of aggression	A	F/C	10
	To identify appropriate strategies for dealing with challenging situations	Dealing with challenging situations scenarios	A	H/O	15
		Sources of stress	A	F/C	10
Approx. total time (mins)					60

*A, activity (participants); F/C, flipchart; H/O, handout; P/I, Post-it notes; T, talk (facilitator)

judo' a tactical communication technique in which 'presence and words' are used to defuse potentially explosive situations and calm difficult people (Horn, 1997; Beckham, 2001; Thompson and Jenkins, 2004; Kokko and Maki, 2009).

Around 10 per cent of your customers can probably be described as 'difficult'. This adjective embraces a range of behaviours, from the demanding to the downright rude. With such customers it is important that you maintain control of not only the situation but also your own emotions. Chapter 9 covers confidence – a trait that should always be cultivated. By staying calm, consistent and confident you will stay in control.

We know that dealing with customers on a day-in day-out basis can be stressful, and that it can be hard to project a helpful, caring attitude – particularly if you're having a bad day. You need to take care of yourself as well as the customers, so this chapter also includes some 'stress-busting' techniques.

Members of staff in front-line services encounter a variety of customers who might be termed difficult. In some instances these customers wish to complain vociferously, and their complaints may or may not be justifiable. Quite often, front-line staff must deal with complaints resulting from situations that have either been created or badly handled by other members of staff. Many difficult situations can be defused before they escalate, but do remember that staff are not paid to be on the receiving end of unwanted attention, harassment or abuse. You have rights too.

Consistency, cooperation and support are important in avoiding difficult situations. It is vital that all staff are familiar with the rules and regulations governing their service, and that they do not bend the rules out of the kindness of their hearts when doing so may have negative repercussions for colleagues, putting them under unnecessary pressure. The main thing is to handle any difficult situation to the best of your abilities in the knowledge that action taken will receive full support from your senior managers, as you have complied with the organisational guidelines.

Dealing with difficult situations can make members of staff feel isolated. No one likes to come across as either unable to cope or lacking in knowledge. It is important that all staff should feel supported by their peers. If a colleague is having difficulty, you can sometimes support them simply by standing alongside them without necessarily intervening. Your very presence may give them the extra confidence to deal with the situation, or give them the option to ask you for help. Anyone in a supervisory role should be aware of what is going on around them, and what may be required of them in terms of potential assistance and support, without necessarily having to be asked.

On the other hand, it is important that staff don't always pass the buck by referring any potentially difficult customer to the supervisory staff. Mutual support engenders a more secure and happy working environment.

Aim 1: To identify behaviours that create positive relationships with customers

Difficult customer consequences

This exercise involves playing a game of consequences using the difficult customer worksheet provided. Each participant answers the first question (from a to c), then folds the paper over and passes it on to the person next to them, who responds to the second question, folds down the paper and passes it on, and so on. This continues until all the questions have been answered.

The participants then divide into two groups, sharing the completed worksheets between them; each group is also given a discussion sheet. Participants will then examine the completed worksheets to derive answers to the questions posed in the discussion sheets.

The worksheet questions are as follows:

1. (a) When I first come into contact with a difficult customer, my usual reaction (thought, response) is:

    (b) As a result of my reaction to a difficult customer, my typical behaviour/response is:

    (c) The consequences of my typical response are:

2. To form a positive relationship with a customer I usually:

3. If a difficult customer perceives me as a friend, the consequences are:

4. If a difficult customer perceives me as threatening, the consequences are:

5. The barriers to establishing a positive relationship with a difficult customer and to providing assistance to such a person are:

6. To be of assistance to someone, I need to think, feel:

7. The best way to establish a positive relationship with another person is to:

8. The most important thing I have learned about customer service as a result of answering these questions is:

The discussion sheet questions are as follows:

1. (a) What patterns of thoughts/feelings can you identify in people's reactions to difficult customers?

    (b) What patterns of actual behaviour/response can you identify?

    (c) What patterns can you identify in the consequences that arise from these responses?

2. What are the barriers to establishing a positive relationship with a difficult customer?

3. What can be done to build bridges instead of barriers?

4. What generalisations can you draw about forming positive relationships with customers?

5. How can you apply what you have learned about dealing with difficult customers?

After the activity, participants may wish to do some self-analysis based on their response to the first question, i.e. 'When I first come in contact with a difficult customer my usual reaction (thought, response) is...'

Some typical reactions (including our own responses) include:

- 'I feel quite churned up inside and tend to give the customer the silent treatment' – This is just plain rude.

- 'I withdraw either physically or psychologically to avoid confrontation, hoping someone else will step in and cope with the situation' – OK, you avoid unpleasantness, but you have landed one of your colleagues with it and also made yourself seem weak.

- 'I use sarcasm or may tend to be aggressive' – You may appear strong and purposeful but could come across as intimidating or even bullying. A response like this invariably makes a bad situation worse.

- 'The customer is always right so I tend to capitulate in order to avoid confrontation' – The customer may be happy but you may have bent the rules, leaving your colleagues open to accusations of unfair treatment in their future service encounters.

- 'I act as if everything is OK and that there will be no escalation of the situation' – This makes you appear lacking in proactivity and ineffectual.

- 'I ignore what is going on as far as I can do in order to avoid confrontation' – This may make you appear easygoing but you may set yourself up as a 'soft touch' for customers.

Participants may also wish to consider how successful or unsuccessful these various reactions are likely to be, and to relate them to the following questions:

- How well do I know my customers and their expectations/needs?

- Am I aware of customer attitudes and behaviours which have the potential to result in a challenging situation?

- How closely do I observe my customers' behaviours in order to identify signs of potentially difficult situations?

- How sensitive am I to non-verbal signals that could alert me to a potentially challenging situation? (Chapter 5)

- What is my usual approach to dealing with challenging situations? How successful is it?

- How assertive am I in challenging situations? (Chapter 9 will help with this.)

- Are there steps that I have taken in the past or might take in the future to minimise the chances of a challenging situation escalating?

- What actions could I take to improve on my current approaches? (Chapter 12 – 'action planning' affords an opportunity to determine these.)

Aim 2: To recognise signs of aggression in a person

Signs of aggression

Before discussing signs of aggression in more detail, the facilitator(s) may wish to ask participants to consider aggressive customers and what signs they might exhibit that could alert staff to their aggression. Thinking back to the chapter on body language might give some clues here. For example:

- agitation, feet shuffling, trembling;
- arms folded defensively;
- boring/glowering, bulging/staring eyes;
- clenched fists;
- exaggerated, faster gestures;
- facial colour – red (flushed) or very pale (white/ashen);
- finger pointing/jabbing;
- muttering to self, gabbling/disjointed speech, swearing;
- purposeful/faster walking;
- raised voice;
- tension in mouth, facial expression;
- tension in upper body.

Other clues might include that the customer:

- bangs their fist or palm on the counter/desk;
- clenches their fists or repeatedly points;
- exhibits bizarre behaviour;
- faces group pressure to be violent or tough (e.g. macho in front of peers);

- has a fast breathing rate;
- has a history of violent actions, attempting previously to hit or throw something at staff;
- has domineering/aggressive body posture;
- invades staff personal space;
- is provocative and name-calling;
- is sweating;
- is uncooperative, has over-sensitive reactions to reasonable requests;
- is under the influence of alcohol, drugs or solvents;
- is verbally abusive – insulting, swearing or making dismissive remarks;
- makes rapid, unpredictable, tense, fidgety movements;
- screws eyes up and has dilated pupils;
- shouts or increases their voice pitch, their tone of voice;
- snaps or replies abruptly with rapid hand movements;
- spits at staff;
- stares and makes uncomfortable eye contact for a long period;
- threatens to use violence or is in possession of a weapon or potential weapon;
- tries to grab hold of, or manhandle, the staff member.

Remember that customers can show aggression in different ways, so there are no hard and fast rules for forecasting aggression. The above signs are nonetheless worth remembering as they can help staff weigh up the risk of customer aggression leading to actual violence. Not all of these are discernible from the previously discussed non-verbal cues, and may in fact relate to internal rather than external factors. This links to the next exercise – considering what might cause a customer to become angry or aggressive. For this, participants should list the causes under two headings – factors internal to the customer and factors external to the customer, i.e. factors caused by other people/situations. This exercise is best performed in two groups, with one group examining internal factors while the other group looks at external factors. Table 8.2 lists factors identified in an actual customer care course. Your participants may come up with others. It is worth noting how many of the outside factors result from avoidable attitudes or actions from staff.

| Table 8.2 | Factors causing customers to become angry/aggressive |

Internal	External
Illness, pain, feeling unwell	Not wanting to lose face in front of peers/members of the opposite sex
Mental health problems	Cultural mis/perception of what constitutes rude or impolite behaviour
Bereavement	Being ignored by staff
Divorce, marital problems	Dismissive action by staff
Alcohol, drugs	Delays in receiving attention/service
Stress of tests, assignments, exams	Queue/line jumping
Stress specific to times of year, e.g. Christmas	Noise
Money worries	Disruptive behaviour of other customers
Hunger, lack of food	Lack of staff availability to help
Lack of knowledge	Perceived lack of helpfulness in staff
Communication difficulties	Perceived lack of interest from staff
Past experience	Tardiness for appointments
Insecurity, feeling threatened, vulnerability	Being criticised or blamed
False or unrealistic expectations	Response to a stressed-out staff member
Personality type – e.g. Type A individuals who are impatient, competitive, workaholics often described as 'stress junkies' who can easily be upset over small things	Copying another customer's response

Aim 3: To identify appropriate strategies for dealing with challenging situations

Handling difficult situations initially involves similar actions to those employed in handling complaints. Remember your ABC:

- *Attend*: pay attention to warning signs.
- *Be calm*: ensure your own body language is reassuring, try to remain controlled and appear confident. Relax your breathing. Slowly and silently count to ten. Do not criticise or confront the customer.

- *Communicate*: use your listening skills to try to understand the signs and needs of the customer; use a firm but friendly tone of voice. Check out the customer's tone and speed of voice.

If the situation is not resolvable, or if you feel you are being insulted, abused or threatened, or that you run the risk of being assaulted, then walk away. Seek help from the appropriate organisational staff, e.g. security personnel. You may need to ask other customers to get help.

If you are assaulted, use minimum force to defend yourself.

Ideally, your organisation will have mechanisms in place to deal with escalated situations. This might include an incident report form to record the incident, any injury, the culprit, and the names and addresses of witnesses.

If you are confronted with a violent situation at work:

- remain calm and level-headed – this may defuse the situation;

- talk to your aggressor, but don't be argumentative;

- don't shout or swear;

- try to contain the situation – don't involve colleagues in the conflict unless absolutely necessary, e.g. the situation has escalated to the point where you feel physically at risk;

- don't be a hero – do not put yourself or others at risk;

- if you are being threatened with a weapon, do exactly what you're told to do;

- get help as soon as the confrontation is over;

- be prepared to experience delayed shock for days or even weeks later;

- remember that violent attacks at work are rare.

Dealing with challenging situations

This exercise involves sample scenarios with challenging situations. It is suggested that you use these if they are a close match to the type of situations in which your participants are likely to find themselves. Facilitators may wish to adapt them to mirror more closely the working conditions and job roles of the participants.

What actions/reactions/responses/solutions are appropriate in the following scenarios?

- You are responsible for issuing new library tickets to fresher students. A new undergraduate arrives to collect her tickets and you have no record of her details. She is very frustrated, interrogates you about your systems and suggests that your service is inefficient. She then turns to her friend and starts complaining loudly about the 'useless' staff in your organisation and how inefficient and ineffective your systems are.

- A very irritated student arrives at your reception area. It seems he has been sent to your section after visiting several other sections. In fact you are unable to deal with his query and are going to have to direct him back to a section to which he has already been.

- You have been trying to get urgent work finished. It is now 9.10 pm and your section closed at 9 pm. A customer is banging on the door seeking urgent attention.

- A student is waiting for help at the reception desk. The phone rings and a member of academic staff simultaneously appears at the desk wanting to speak to you.

- A senior member of the profession who is addressing a workshop at your organisation tomorrow rings from one of the local hotels. She is demanding an explanation of why there is no booking in her name despite being informed there would be. She was also expecting to have a workshop briefing pack available for her on her arrival.

- An internal customer arrives, complaining that she has left several requests for your colleagues in a different section to phone her, but she has heard nothing and it is now urgent. You are aware that the message has been passed to the other section but that they don't see the task as a priority. No one from the section is available at present.

- Although the library building officially closes at 10 pm on a Saturday, the short-loan desk closes 15 minutes earlier to give the staff sufficient time to deal with the queue that inevitably forms because students can borrow the items for the whole of Sunday and need not return them until 10 am on Monday. A student arrives at 9.50 pm and demands that you bend the rules to accommodate them as they were held up in traffic en route to the library. He also claims that one of your colleagues let him take out an item at the same time last weekend.

- To be able to borrow valuable materials, members of the library (whether staff or students) must produce valid identification in the form of a library borrower card. A customer who claims to be a senior member of academic staff, but who is unknown to you, and does not have his card with him, wishes to borrow one of your rare books. He expects you to make an exception in his case because of his status.

- The library is testing a new copier/scanner. To check its durability and reliability it has been put on open access and customers are allowed to copy or scan documents at no charge. As a consequence, there is a long line of customers waiting to avail themselves of this special service. An argument has broken out between two customers. It unclear whether this is because someone has been using the machine for too long or whether someone is being accused of queue jumping. One customer claims that another customer threw a stapler at him during the row.

- To relieve pressure on counter/desk staff, customers are generally encouraged to use the self-service check-out/issue system as often as possible. A customer who you have shown how to use the self-service system on numerous occasions still insists on coming to you and asking for help. You have also witnessed her approaching other staff members and you know they too have explained the system to her before. She approaches you at a particularly busy time and asks for help self-issuing her books

- Two students are in a queue for items for the reserve book collection. Two members of staff serve them simultaneously. One member of staff engages in brief welcoming conversation with the first person in the line while the second staff member just goes straight to the shelves. As it happens, both students want the sole remaining copy of a particular set text. When the first student sees that the second student has been given the text, he points out that he was actually ahead of that student in the queue.

As is usual with scenario exercises, there are no right and wrong answers, but in many of the above scenarios and other potentially difficult situations, a simple but courteous statement can eliminate the need for elaborate explanations, for example:

- We don't provide that service.

- No, that is not possible.

- I have served you to the best of my ability. Now I have to get on with my work/serve the next borrower.

Remember that you need to make a negative response clear and unambiguous. You are more likely to be challenged if you appear unsure or tentative. Do not, for example, use phrases such as:

- I don't think that would be possible.

- That is against our usual policy.

Such phrases can give customers the impression that it might be worth pursuing their request.

If you are unsure about the rules/regulations, you may wish to check with a colleague or supervisor – but make sure you read up on the rules afterwards.

If a customer is really persistent, you may have to resort to something along the following lines:

> I will not discuss this any more unless you have some new information about the situation. If you do, please write it down for me and I will decide whether it seems reasonable to talk about it again.

Many of the situations described above are similar to the potentially negative customer-to-customer interactions described by Rowley (1995), who highlights the need for library staff (and managers in particular) to consider what can be done to positively influence the way customers can affect each other. Rowley reviews roles of customer compatibility management, including the legislator who 'creates a compatible service environment through the enactment of rules and policies that guide the behaviour of patrons' and the teacher, who passes on 'information that is intended to either: instil expectations or norms ... or educate the customer with respect to how to use the service' (Rowley, 1995: 10–11)

The previously discussed game of consequences will have given participants an opportunity to say how they feel when dealing with difficult customers. Dealing with a difficult situation may leave you feeling angry, hurt or upset. It is helpful if staff have the chance to talk over such situations rather than bottling things up. It is useful to talk over situations in order to know how best to deal with them. Discussing the mini case studies should help participants with this. In addition, we discuss stress and stress-busting methods below.

Stress

Anyone seeking to find out just how stressed they are can read a multitude of books on the subject and take any number of tests. Stress is something experienced by most people, and the present authors are no exception. One of us was undergoing a management training course which involved taking a stress-rating exercise that allocated points for stressful life events. Participants were told that one in five people whose lives had changed significantly during the course of a 12-month period could expect to suffer a major illness within the next two years. They were also told that 80 per cent of those who scored more than 300 points, and 50 per cent of those who scored between 150 and 300 points were likely to become clinically depressed, suffer a heart attack or some other serious illness. In the space of three months, the author had experienced:

- divorce (score 73);
- marital separation (score 65);
- a change in health of a family member (score 44);
- a personal business readjustment (score 39);
- change to a different line of work (score 36);
- son leaving home (score 29);
- trouble with the in-laws (score 29);
- a move of home (score 20).

On top of these were other stress-inducing events that did not even appear on the list. Needless to say, just seeing the results of the test did nothing to reduce an already impressive score of 335. However, she has survived this remarkable stress level, and some 15 years later, is still fit, healthy and enjoying life!

In short, we don't want to be doom-laden. We would just like to help you recognise the symptoms, signals and sources of stress, and to suggest some tactics you might deploy to help overcome or at least cope with your stress.

Recognising sources of stress

For this exercise, participants should work in pairs for five minutes to discuss possible sources of stress at work. At the end of the exercise, participants may call out the answers which can then be written onto a flipchart.

The following responses were from participants at a customer care course:

- achieving work–life balance;
- commuting difficulties, traffic jams affecting punctuality;
- coping with change;
- difficult, uncooperative colleagues;

- expectations of yourself and of others;
- having a demanding line manager;
- having a desk that looks like a bombsite – too much paperwork;
- having a task that is over-demanding, that you don't know how to tackle;
- having to work at a high speed for long periods;
- having to work through lunch and other breaks to meet deadlines;
- having too many responsibilities as well as too many restrictions;
- having too much to do, being overwhelmed by your 'to do' list;
- inefficiencies in other departments/sections of the organisation;
- pressure of decision-making;
- red tape and bureaucracy that appear to stop you doing your job;
- rude customers;
- taking work home with you, whether physically or mentally (e.g. not being able to switch off, lying awake worrying about work-related matters);
- trying to maintain standards, being true to your own values/beliefs;
- work and personal relationships;
- working environment and physical conditions (heating, lighting, telephones).

On top of such work-related stress, we often also import stress from our private lives into the workplace. Such stress may stem from personal or family issues, health, money matters, or a variety of other 'slings and arrows' that are too numerous to mention. Regardless of whether our stress is directly related to work or a response to personal issues, our physical and emotional responses remain the same, and the 'stress-busting' techniques discussed later in this chapter are valid for all types of stress.

Our initial response to stress is physical – this is a natural reaction that prepares humans for fighting or fleeing. Continued stimulation of these reactions brings about adverse symptoms (see Table 8.3) and can damage health in the long run.

Our response to stress is not just physical, but also mental and behavioural. Mental responses include:

- apathy, feeling of pointlessness, nothing matters;
- depression, guilt, loneliness, moodiness;

Table 8.3   Physical responses to stress

Physical reaction	Symptom
Brain sends biochemical message to the pituitary gland, releasing adrenocorticotropic hormone, triggering adrenal gland	Headaches/migraine Dizziness
Pupils dilate so they can see better in dim light	Blurred vision
Mouth goes dry	Difficulty swallowing
Neck and shoulder muscles tense – large skeletal muscles contract ready for action	Aching neck Backache
Breathing becomes faster and shallower, supplying more oxygen to muscles	Over-breathing/hyperventilation Chest pains Tingling Palpitations Asthma
Heart pumps faster and blood pressure rises	High blood pressure
Liver releases stored sugar to provide fuel for quick energy	Excess sugar in blood Indigestion
Digestion slows down or changes as blood is diverted away from the stomach to muscles of arms and legs to fight or run away	Nausea, indigestion ulcers, dyspepsia, gastric symptoms
Body cools itself by perspiring; blood vessels and capillaries move close to skin surface ready for vigorous physical action	Excess sweating Blushing
Muscles at opening of anus and bladder are relaxed	Frequent urination, diarrhoea

- distorted, irrational ideas, jealousy;
- feeling of 'cracking up', loss of control;
- forgetfulness;
- inability to make decisions;
- lack of concentration;
- nervousness, feeling of being 'wound up';

- reduced self-esteem, negative attitude to self, loss of confidence;
- sudden feelings of fear or panic;
- worrying something awful will happen, worst-possible scenarios.

Behavioural responses to stress include:

- accident-proneness;
- avoidance of anxiety-provoking situations;
- excessive drinking/smoking/drug taking;
- increase in obsessional tendencies, e.g. about cleanliness, illness, food;
- increased irritability, edginess and bad temper;
- irregular eating habits (overeating or loss of appetite);
- loss of libido;
- manic increase in activity level;
- social withdrawal, putting off seeing friends, no longer engaging in sports/hobbies, becoming introverted;
- trouble getting to sleep at night/early waking/tiredness/exhaustion/lethargy.

Not only can individuals be stressed, but groups and organisations can experience stress too. Successful teambuilding (Chapter 11) can minimise group stress, but it may be worth touching upon some symptoms of group stress at this stage. Group stress symptoms include:

- atmosphere of distrust;
- few people contribute to discussions;
- group members work in isolation and not as a group;
- high level of absenteeism;
- high level of job dissatisfaction;
- high level of non-assertive behaviour, e.g. opting out;
- high levels of aggressive behaviour;
- high staff turnover;
- lack of mutual respect;
- low morale;
- low trust, high dissatisfaction, poor problem-solving;
- mistakes used to punish people;
- no review of progress on issues or how the group is working;

- no sharing of common problems;
- psychological game playing and politicking;
- unhealthy competition.

Advice on stress-busting

Look for sources of stress, and analyse potentially stressful situations for ways of avoiding them. Know your stress points. Consider if there are certain factors in your working life that you might alter to make your job less stressful and more rewarding. The following are offered as potential solutions to stressful situations. There is no hard and fast rule. Different people find different ways of handling stress.

- Try to get organised if you feel that your stress is caused by work overload. Consider making a master plan or 'to do' list in which you group similar tasks into manageable sections and then prioritise. Breaking a big task into smaller sections or 'eating an elephant with a teaspoon' can alleviate anxiety (action planning in Chapter 12 may help here).

- Don't procrastinate, i.e. don't do all the jobs you like doing first when they are the least important on your 'to do' list. Rule an A4 sheet into two and head one half 'Imperative' (must be done today) and the other half 'Important' (need to be done sometime this week). The imperative list should not contain more than four things in total but it must be completed by the end of the day. Get real and get on with what has to be done first. You will feel much better about your day and achieve so much more.

- If your desk looks like a bombsite, spend some time sorting everything out. Whatever happened to the paperless office? Each piece of paper should pass through your hands once only. It should be dealt with, discarded or delegated.

- Learn to organise your time effectively, manage your time rather than letting others manage it for you. Do you get lieu time or comp time for the extra hours you work? Can you negotiate an early finish once a week in return for an early start?

- Know your limitations. Don't be overambitious, setting yourself impossibly high standards. Avoid trying to be Superman or Wonder Woman. Learn to delegate, learn to say 'no'.

- Don't take all criticisms as absolute truth. Don't take them personally. Allow yourself to make mistakes – nobody is perfect.

- Remember how in Chapter 5 (Table 5.3) we discussed replacing negative words with positive ones? You can do this when you are thinking about yourself, shifting your focus from your failures to your successes. For example, replace 'I can't do that' with 'I have not yet learned how to do that – but I will'. Recognise negative thinking and try to regain objectivity in order to develop a more positive attitude. With practice, you can alter your thinking patterns to more positive ones. Develop more trust in yourself and in your colleagues.

- Don't worry about factors beyond your control.

- Relax and put so-called crises into perspective. It may be a cliché, but try to see them as challenges or opportunities and look for unusual or creative solutions.

- Give and receive praise and recognition to colleagues. Hopefully they will reciprocate.

- Value your network of friends, acquaintances and colleagues. Try to find someone to whom you can speak openly about your feelings when you are angry or worried. Learn to express these feelings rather than bottle them up.

- Discharge anger as quickly (and safely!) as possible. Then analyse what happened to make you angry.

- Whether or not you have a family member, friend or colleague with whom you can share your feelings, you may find it useful to keep a diary record, e.g. times you felt angry or frustrated and what triggered such reactions. This can help you change your pattern. If you can write about how you feel, this can defuse these negative feelings, and you may find that by 'offloading' them in your diary, you are spending less time obsessing about them in your head.

- If you are feeling frustrated by customers, try to make a game out of your frustration by making an internal tally of their quirks, foibles and eccentricities. At the same time, cut them some slack – you don't know their personal circumstances. They may be experiencing even more stress than you.

- The next time a customer is driving you to distraction, take a deep breath and let it out. Think of yourself as breathing out tension and breathing in calm.

- After a stressful encounter, do some stress-busting exercises (e.g. those mentioned in the section on energisers in Chapter 2).

If your line manager is excessively demanding, Chapter 9 on confidence and assertiveness may help you to deal with this. If you feel you are being picked upon, consider how far any criticisms are justified, consider what you might do or what your line manager might do to make adjustments, and try to find an appropriate opportunity to discuss issues.

If your line manager or a colleague criticises you, take a deep breath and practise some active listening. Try to find out why they voiced the criticism. It may not be true, but they may perceive it as true. As such, you need either to address the situation or find out how to change their perception. You might want to consult a trusted colleague for a second opinion. When someone points out that you are not perfect, bear in mind that you are in good company.

If you are sitting for long periods at work, use rest breaks or quieter moments to do some simple stretches to release muscle tension, for example:

- shrug your shoulders;
- turn your head slowly from left to right and stretch back gently at the same time;
- do a full body stretch by reaching up towards the ceiling;
- stretch out your arms and move your fingers up and down.

Retain your sense of proportion and your sense of humour. Accept that some days you're the pigeon, and some days you're the statue.

Compartmentalise work and non-work activity. Don't take work home literally or metaphorically. With respect to non-work activity, think about the things that really make you happy and concentrate on these. This should help to positively reinforce your life outside of work, and encourage you to make the time to enjoy it.

Further tips for healthy-living include:

- eat at least one hot, balanced meal a day;
- limit your alcohol consumption – for women, the limit is 2–3 units a day, for men it is 3–4 units a day (*www.drinkaware.co.uk*);
- drink no more than three cups of coffee (or any other caffeinated drink) a day;
- try to maintain a healthy weight for your height;
- keep smoking/pill-taking habits under control;
- try to get 7–8 hours sleep at least four nights a week;

- increase your level of physical fitness – get off the bus a stop early and walk the rest of the way to work;
- have regular check-ups, e.g. dental, eye tests and hearing tests;
- take some quiet time and relaxation for yourself during the day – read for pleasure, listen to music, do a crossword, take up yoga, walk the dog, do some gardening;
- try to do something 'fun' at least once a week – attend clubs, social activities, etc.

Case study: a bad day at the office

The Metropolitan Central Library is located within the centre of a large city, close to the main shopping area and transport hubs. It is an exceptionally busy facility, and its readily accessible coffee shop, newspaper lounge and rest rooms make it an attractive venue for a variety of visitors to the city centre.

One of the subject librarians is a fanatical theatre buff, and has an encyclopaedic knowledge of the history of the local theatre. Her favourite customer is a retired minor actor, whose main claim to fame is that he briefly appeared in a well-known soap opera on television, and at the height of his fame, as a 'local lad made good', was invited to switch on the Christmas lights in the town centre. He also claims to have known a certain, now-ennobled actress 'rather well'. Despite his limited fame, this librarian treats him as if he were a Hollywood star, and literally cannot do enough for him. She has spoon-fed him to the extent that even if he were capable of doing things for himself, he has now become so used to having everything done for him, that his 'learned helplessness' is probably now a permanent fixture.

If the librarian is on duty when he comes in, she will interrupt whatever she is doing for the 'honour' of serving him. Unfortunately, she is not always there, and he has come to expect the same 'regal' treatment from whoever happens to be on duty at the time. Moreover, if he does not get this same level of service he can become quite difficult. This recently culminated in a situation where he was extremely rude to a young library assistant who had merely politely explained that the level of service that he was requesting – to check the catalogue to see if six books were on the shelves, and then to actually go and collect them for him – was beyond that which was routinely provided for an able-bodied customer.

Analysis

By providing this 'preferred customer' with a unique level of customer service, this librarian has not only misled him into accepting that such treatment is 'the norm', but more importantly, in so doing has condemned her fellow-workers to the thankless task of constantly appearing to fail to deliver this 'normal' service. Thus, both the customer and staff are joint losers in this unhappy arrangement, which could so easily have been avoided had the librarian made it very clear from the outset that either:

- what she was providing him as a 'one-off' personal favour was far and above the normal level of service; or

- she could not provide the level of service that he was asking for, as it was so preferential that it could not possibly be extended to every customer – and that would be unfair to all.

The situation is not only frustrating for fellow library staff, but the strange relationship has also become a laughing matter, to the detriment of the reputation and the standing of both the subject librarian and her favoured customer, who are now referred to as Dame Cecily and Sir Larry.

Additional points

When agreeing to go the extra mile for someone, make sure (in a pleasant manner) that they know that you are doing so.

If you do 'go that extra mile', don't be surprised if your customer subsequently says to one of your colleagues that 'so and so did this for me...' Where you have a particularly 'needy' customer, use a staff meeting to discuss your approach to them. It is important that your response is both consistent and fair, that all staff understand what the preferred approach is to be, and that they then apply it as agreed.

This type of incident is so common that there really should be some written guidelines as to what the 'normal level of service' is as regards retrieving books from shelves etc. Such guidelines are particularly important for new, inexperienced, or perhaps just under-confident staff.

Do not allow such situations to fester. This may well be a source of some amusement, but it is also potentially divisive in terms of the library 'team'. Moreover, the customer is also being misled, and his 'skewed' assessment of the service he is being offered by this one librarian has made him believe that the general level of service on offer is 'below par'.

Be aware that 'close personal attention' may also be misinterpreted by some – the customer in question eventually misinterpreted the librarian's close personal attention as some sort of romantic interest. He wrote her a letter of a very personal nature which subsequently proved deeply embarrassing for all concerned. He no longer visits the library, and the librarian in question has now over-corrected, and is in danger of appearing very aloof and disconnected from her customers. Balance is required in all things…

Further reading

Alothen, G. and Gross, V. (1991) 'Saying "no" to foreign students', in C. Lago (ed.) *Working with Overseas Students: A Staff Development Manual.* Huddersfield: University of Huddersfield/British Council, pp. 333–7.

Berckhan, B. (2001) *Judo with Words: An Intelligent Way to Counter Verbal Attacks*, London: Free Association.

Friedman, M. and Rosenman, R. H. (1974) *Type A Behavior and Your Heart*, New York: Knopf.

Friedman, M. (1996) *Type A Behavior: Its Diagnosis and Treatment*, New York: Plenum Press.

Gardner, C.A. (2005) 'The importance of customer service', *Virginia Libraries* 51(4): 2–4.

Horn, S. (1997) *Tongue Fu*, New York: St Martins Press.

Kean, C. and McKoy-Johnson, F. (2009) 'Patron aggression in the academic library: A study of the Main Library at the University of the West Indies, Mona', *New Library World* 110(7/8): 373–84.

Kokko, T. and Maki, M. (2009) 'The verbal judo approach in demanding customer encounters', *Services Marketing Quarterly* 30(3): 212–33.

Lark, S. (2004) *Anxiety and Stress: A Self-Help Programme* (rev edn), Berkeley, CA: Celestial Arts.

McGrath, H. and Goulding, A. (1996) 'Part of the job: violence in public libraries', *New Library World* 97(1127): 4–13.

Osa, J. O. (2002) 'The difficult patron situation: competency-based training to empower frontline staff', *The Reference Librarian* 38 (75/76): 263–76.

Plant, J. and Stephenson, J. (2009) *Beating Stress, Anxiety and Depression: Groundbreaking Ways to Help You Feel Better*, London: Piatkus.

Powell, T. (1997) *Free Yourself from Harmful Stress*, London: Dorling Kindersley.

Rowley, J. (1995) 'Customer compatibility management, or revisiting the silence rule', *Library Review* 44(4/5): 7–12.

Rubin, R. J. (2000) 'Diffusing [sic] the angry patron', available at: *http://www .westga.edu/~library/depts/circ/proc/Diffusing%20the%20Angry%20Patron. pdf* (accessed 24 September 2009).

Sams, A. (2009) *Check out: A Life on the Tills*, London: Gallic.

Sarkodie-Mensah, K. (2002) *Helping the Difficult Library Patron: New Approaches to Examining and Resolving a Long-Standing and Ongoing Problem*, New York: Haworth Information Press.

Smith, K. (1994) *Serving the Difficult Customer: A How-To-Do-It Manual for Library Staff*, New York: Neal Schuman.

Stress Tips. Available at: *http://www.stresstips.com* (accessed 23 September 2009).

Thompson, G. J. and Jenkins, J. B. (2004) *Verbal Judo: The Gentle Art of Persuasion*, New York: Quill.

US Office of Personnel Management (1998) 'Dealing with workplace violence: a guide for agency planners', available at: *http://www.opm.gov/Employment_and_Benefits/WorkLife/OfficialDocuments/handbooksguides/WorkplaceViolence/p1-s3.asp* (accessed 23 September 2009).

Life positions and the OK Corral: being more confident and assertive

No one can make you feel inferior without your consent. (Eleanor Roosevelt)

Being assertive is essentially about respecting yourself and others. It is about having a basic belief that your opinions, beliefs, thoughts and feelings are as important as anybody else's – and that this goes for other people too. It is about being in touch with your own needs and wants, but contrary to some misconceptions about assertive behaviour, it is not about going for what you want at any cost. (Shan Rees and Roderick S. Graham)

Being assertive means being honest with yourself and others. It means having the ability to say directly what it is you want, you need or you feel, but not at the expense of other people. It means having confidence in yourself and being positive, while at the same time understanding other people's point of view. It means being able to behave in a rational and adult way. Being assertive means being able to negotiate and reach workable compromises. Above all, being assertive means having self-respect and respect for other people. (Rennie Fritchie)

Aims

The aims of this chapter are as follows:

- to recognise aggressive, assertive, adaptive and apathetic styles of behaviour;
- to use assertive language in response to customer and staff statements.

To assist with planning, Table 9.1 presents a suggested session plan.

| Table 9.1 | Session plan – OK Corral and life positions – being more confident and assertive |

Session	Aims	Content	Methods	Aids	Time (mins)
OK Corral and life positions: being more confident and assertive	To recognise aggressive, assertive, adaptive and apathetic styles of behaviour		T		10
		Confidence blocks	A	F/C	10
		Influencing styles	A	H/O	20
	To use assertive language in response to customer and staff statements	Assertiveness quizzes	A	H/O	10
		OK Corral scenarios		H/O F/C	20
Approx. total time (mins)					70

*A, activity (participants); F/C, flipchart; H/O, handout; P/I, Post-it notes; T, talk (facilitator)

Background

This chapter deals with two concepts: confidence and assertiveness. The chapter is essentially about personal presence and the ability to present that confident persona which makes assertiveness techniques so effective. It is quite possible that the facilitators do not feel sufficiently confident themselves to conduct this section of the course and they may wish to omit it. On the other hand, they might want to consider what our two-year-old granddaughter recently said to her mother: 'Mummy, me too small for today'.

We all have days when we feel overwhelmed by people, systems and things seemingly beyond our control, where we experience crises of confidence. An under-confident facilitator may be suffering from the impostor syndrome, perhaps thinking that they are not up to delivering the goods. Think back to the first few chapters and the hints and tips about communication and dealing with stressful situations. All these should help to develop real and lasting self-confidence.

So where does confidence come from? Frequently it is reserved for situations in which you have previously had successes, or because other people, family, friends or colleagues have given you positive strokes in the form of encouragement or of recognition for a job well done. If you are truly confident, you will feel empowered to try out new experiences without getting overly stressed or anxious. True confidence comes from within and requires us to quash defeatist behaviour, attitudes and thoughts.

Confidence can be undermined by implicit value judgments about ourselves. These may involve judging ourselves, e.g 'I am doing a terrible job', or perceptions of how others are judging us, e.g. 'They think I am doing a terrible job'. These judgments may also be based on perceptions that 'They are doing a better job than me...' Modesty is a virtue in our culture and it is considered big-headed to blow your own trumpet. In a later chapter, we challenge this way of thinking by asking participants to celebrate their own successes and to tell people what they are good at. So, as far as this chapter is concerned, being overly modest can come across as lacking self-confidence.

When embarking on a new course of action (e.g. facilitating a customer care course), think of yourself as being self-aware rather than self-conscious. Self-consciousness can result in focusing on yourself rather than on others, and in not reading those crucial signs we discussed in the communication chapter. Self-awareness involves acknowledging your own feelings and those of others so that you can act appropriately in given situations.

If you anticipate negative outcomes when in an unfamiliar situation, this is often a self-fulfilling prophecy. If you repeat the pattern, you are in danger of achieving an unhappy state of 'learned helplessness', where any positive outcome becomes most unlikely. A much better starting point when entering any new situation is to anticipate a range of possible outcomes. Giving yourself permission to make mistakes is important. Do the best you can, and go into things with a willingness to learn and to change.

The first activity in this session concerns 'confidence blocks'. At the end of the session, participants are *not* required to report back on the confidence blocks they have discussed with a trusted partner. However, it would be useful to know how they felt about participating in the activity.

Reassure them that confidence takes time to build up and that it can be knocked back by life's experiences. Ideally, the course will help them to be more confident in communicating, in defusing charged situations, and in dealing with confrontation and conflict. This chapter includes a guide to developing confidence that can be given to participants after the confidence blocks exercise.

Aim 1: To recognise aggressive, assertive, adaptive and apathetic styles of behaviour

Developing confidence

Self-confidence involves the ability to feel confident about yourself in the face of resistance, uncertainty, conflict or pressure. Self-confidence is based on acceptance of self, not on feelings of superiority towards other people. Remember:

- you cannot give someone self-confidence, but you can help an individual become aware of their own level of self-confidence;
- self-confidence is the key to assertive behaviour;
- we often assume that we lose confidence due to other people's actions or their judgments of us. In reality, however, confidence is actually *given away*.

To develop self-confidence, we must give up self-defeating behaviours that undermine confidence, such as those in the first column of Table 9.2, and take steps to build up beneficial self-influencing behaviours such as those in the second column.

Table 9.2 Self-influencing behaviours

Negative	Positive
Putting yourself down implicitly/explicitly	Be aware of your own level of confidence
Letting others put you down	Recognise your own ability, what you are good at
Perceiving others as having qualities you don't possess	Accept your own needs, thoughts and feelings
Looking at your weaknesses and others' strengths	Trust your feelings as a guide to action
Anticipating the worst possible scenario	Anticipate a variety of possibilities
Not letting go of past failures	Give yourself permission to get things wrong sometimes
Expecting perfection in yourself	Look after yourself, and remember that no one is perfect
Expecting others to confirm your lack of self-confidence	Pay attention to your breathing and your posture, and think positively

Table 9.2   Self-influencing behaviours (*Cont'd*)

Negative	Positive
Expecting criticisms/judgments from others to confirm your own negative self-image	Celebrate your (and your team's) successes
Not accepting compliments, e.g. being cynical about them	Accept and enjoy compliments
Holding back feelings when you receive a compliment, e.g. not being pleased	Compliment yourself for a good job well done, and express your thanks
Being self-judgmental, self-critical	Encourage yourself to be the best that you can be
Not believing in yourself, e.g. that you are not good at your job	Actively look for support from others, e.g. recognition, acceptance, training

Confidence blocks

This activity provides an opportunity for participants to explore how they may undermine their own confidence, and to identify appropriate action to avoid sabotaging themselves.

Each participant should choose a partner from the group, preferably someone with whom they are happy or at ease. From the outset, participants should be reassured that they do not have to report back on this task.

Individually, participants should think of a recent occasion when they felt they lacked the confidence to deal effectively with a situation. They should then write down brief details of the event, such as the situation, who was involved, and their feelings, thoughts and judgments about themselves.

When both participants in the pair are ready, they should take it in turns to talk through the situation, using their partner to clarify the *specific* behaviours and thoughts they may have used to undermine themselves (e.g. believing that they could not cope or that the other person was more powerful).

In the light of this analysis, participants should consider what they might do or to say to themselves in a similar situation in the future.

Participants should share equally the time available so that everyone has the same opportunity to identify particular strategies for developing confidence.

Assertiveness

What is assertiveness?

How do you get customers to behave as you would like without entering into conflict or being aggressive or overly officious? Where and how should you draw the line between being of service and being servile? Assertive behaviour is one of the most important skills for the twenty-first century workforce as it means that staff can put forward ideas in a way that is effective while having regard for the needs of others – whether they are line managers, colleagues or customers. Development of such skills can have a far-reaching impact on an organisation by:

- improving internal communications and teamwork;
- promoting better relationships with customers;
- empowering staff to put forward ideas and to express opinions;
- improving staff motivation and raising staff morale.

Assertiveness is sometimes associated with aggressiveness, but they are two quite different behaviour types. Aggressive behaviour involves standing up for your rights to the extent that you violate the rights of others, expressing thoughts and feelings in inappropriate ways, believing that your own thoughts and feelings are more important than those of others, and even being contemptuous of others. On the other hand, assertive behaviour involves standing up for yourself in a way that does not violate the rights of others, and honestly and openly expressing your viewpoint while, at the same time, showing you understand other people's position.

Submissive behaviour involves failure to stand up for yourself by expressing thoughts and feelings in apologetic or self-effacing ways or, indeed, by failing to express them at all.

The influencing styles questionnaire

This questionnaire enables an analysis of different behaviour styles (including assertiveness and aggressiveness) and their effect on ourselves and on others. If appropriate to the group, make a quadrant on a flipchart page, and label the four sections as aggressive, adaptive, apathetic and assertive. Once participants have completed and scored the questionnaire, they can then enter their name in the section that represents the style for which they got their highest score. Alternatively, facilitators may prefer to distribute informational handouts giving characteristics that map onto the different styles.

The questionnaire is adapted from The Solicitors' Coach Assertiveness Profile, available at: *http://www.thesolicitorscoach.co.uk/phdi/p1.nsf/ pages/ 1801:AssertivenessProfile.pdf/$file/AssertivenessProfile.pdf* (accessed 23 October 2009).

The questionnaire

This questionnaire is designed to help you identify the different ways in which you think and feel about yourself and others, and behave towards them. The results of the questionnaire will give you an indication of some of your preferred ways of influencing others.

There are 80 statements. Respond with *yes* if the statement is like or true of you by highlighting, or putting a tick against, the statement

Respond to the statements as spontaneously and honestly as you can. The more honest you are with yourself, the more relevant and significant your results will be.

Working at a steady pace, it usually takes approximately 5–10 minutes to complete the questionnaire. Do not take too long thinking about your responses.

I often...

1. assume I won't get what I want
2. don't know what I want when I am asked
3. expect that other people will dislike me
4. experience difficulty in getting close to other people
5. fantasise about ways of getting my own back on other people
6. feel angry towards other people
7. feel hostile towards other people
8. feel hurt by other people
9. feel miserable
10. feel resentful towards other people
11. feel that other people have let me down
12. get short-tempered with people
13. get despondent about things in general
14. have negative thoughts about myself and other people
15. receive acknowledgment from other people for what I do
16. suspect other people's motives
17. think other people are after something when they thank me

I usually...

18. ask questions in order to gather information
19. assume that I won't get what I want
20. assume that other people will not get on with me
21. deal directly with conflict situations
22. enjoy discussing ideas with people
23. enjoy getting involved with, and committed to, tasks
24. exercise caution about what I say to other people about myself
25. experience difficulty in delegating to other people
26. express my feelings openly towards other people
27. feel anxious about upsetting other people
28. feel equal to other people
29. feel guilty when I refuse a request
30. feel inferior to other people
31. find it difficult to sort out my problems
32. go along with what other people want
33. let other people make decisions for me
34. listen to, and take account of, other people's views
35. rely on other people to take decisions for me
36. respect other people irrespective of their views
37. *tell* people rather than ask them to do things
38. tell people what I think
39. think I am the only one who can do the job correctly
40. try to spot the flaws in other people' arguments

I generally...

41. avoid taking on responsibility
42. check out my assumptions with the people concerned
43. deal indirectly with conflict situations
44. enjoy getting on with my work
45. give people no choice when I ask for what I want
46. have a sense of wellbeing

47. have creative solutions to problems

48. say sorry when I have made a mistake

49. take account of other people's needs and wants

50. try not to offend other people

I regularly...

51. appreciate other people for what they have done

52. feel de-motivated in my work

53. seek feedback from other people

54. seek other people' views when making decisions which affect them

I rarely...

55. ask for what I want

56. give praise to other people

57. receive feedback about my behaviour

58. say 'no' when asked to do something

59. tell other people what I really think or feel

I am ready to...

60. accept that people will sometimes say 'no' to me

61. criticise other people

62. feel subject to criticism

63. take on responsibility

I tend to...

64. avoid eye contact

65. be anxious about what other people think of me

66. be inconsistent about what I tell people

67. be put upon by other people

68. be quick to put down other people's ideas

69. be sarcastic

70. blame other people when things go wrong

71. dismiss other people's wants and needs

72. feel lonely

73. jump to and draw conclusions

74. keep myself to myself

75. let other people take responsibility for me

76. mistrust other people

77. prefer other people to take the lead and for me to follow

78. put myself down

79. see other people as more important than me

80. think that other people are better than me

Scoring instructions

1. Circle all the numbers on the scoring chart (Table 9.3) to which you have responded *yes* by highlighting or ticking the statement.

2. Score one point for each *yes* you have circled.

Table 9.3   Scoring chart for influencing styles questionnaire

Aggressive	Adaptive	Apathetic	Assertive
1	2	4	15
6	3	5	18
10	8	7	21
11	19	9	22
12	27	13	23
25	29	14	26
37	30	16	28
38	32	17	34
39	33	20	36
40	35	24	42
45	50	31	44
56	55	41	46
57	58	43	47
61	65	52	48
62	67	59	49
68	75	64	51
70	77	66	53
71	78	69	54
73	79	72	60
76	80	74	63

3. Add up and total your scores for each of the vertical columns in Table 9.3.

4. The total for each column shows your preference for each of the four styles of influencing.

5. Read the notes on interpreting your scores and the descriptions of your highest and lowest influencing style scores (Table 9.4).

Table 9.4	Influencing styles characteristics

	Aggressive	Adaptive	Apathetic	Assertive
Feelings	Arrogant, confrontational, dismissive, indignant, irritated, self-righteous, sarcastic, cynical, superior, directive, judgmental, a 'control freak', blaming, hostile, rigid, critical, persistent, picky, exacting, moralistic, manipulative, authoritarian, power-oriented, competitive	Holding self in low esteem, lacking confidence, conciliatory, helpless, embarrassed, shameful, guilty, anxious, sense of inferiority complex, meek, dependent, inadequate, nervous, apologetic, pliable, conforming, awkward, unsure, a 'doormat'	Holding self in low esteem, lacking confidence, harbouring negative feelings about self and others, suspicious, inferiority complex, inadequate, hurt, fearful, anxious, guilty, passive, withdrawing, retreating 'into a shell', suppressing feelings, de-motivated, depressed, feeling of despair, rejection, reserved, sullen	Confident in self and others, high self-esteem, interested, motivated, persuasive, energetic, proactive, standing up for self, alert, stimulating, enthusiastic, focused, level-headed, decisive, independent, practical, efficient, synergistic and cooperative
Eyes	Glaring, frowning, narrowed-eyes trying to stare down, expressionless, severe eye contact	Evasive, darting, avoiding eye contact, looking down or up	Avoiding eye contact, staring into space	Direct, open, steady but not staring eye contact

| Table 9.4 | Influencing styles characteristics (Cont'd) |

	Aggressive	Adaptive	Apathetic	Assertive
Hands/ posture/ gestures	Finger-pointing, jerky movements, fists thumping, clenched fists, arms crossed, hands on hips, striding around impatiently, stands upright with head 'in the air', stiff rigid posture	Hand-wringing, round hunching shoulders, covering mouth with hand, nervous movements, hesitant gestures, stepping backwards or sideways, biting lips, adjusting clothing	Downcast head slumped, shrugs and shuffles, arms crossed for protection, moving away, self-effacing, slow, low energy movements, hesitant gestures, covering mouth with hands, unresponsive, distracted fiddling, limited use of gestures, fewer facial expressions	Open hand movements, measured pace of movements, relaxed sympathetic gestures, standing comfortably but grounded firmly on two feet, steady, straight posture, head held up, hands loose at sides
Mouth	Scowls, jaw set firm, chin thrust forward, eyebrows raised in disbelief, 'wry' smile	Unreal smiles when angry or being criticised, eyebrows raised in anticipation, quick changing features	Usually unsmiling, blank expression, pathetic or unreal smiles, jaw loose	Open features, steady, relaxed but not loose jaw, smiles when pleased, frowns when angry
Speech	Using strong, direct language, trying to overpower customer with speech, interrupting, ignoring responses, relentlessly demanding, shouting, sarcastic, threatening, judgmental harsh, cold controlling tone,	Wobbly, whining or singsong, over-soft or over-warm, rambling, hesitant (allowing interruptions), lots of pauses, modifiers ('quite', 'slightly'), quiet, drops away at the end, throat clearing frequently, jerks from fast to slow *'You'll probably think I'm silly but...'*	Saying little, dull, meek monotone, whining, pleading, apologetic, mumbling, rambling, hesitant, quiet, flat, frequent silences, long pauses (allowing interruptions), meaning unclear, confusing sentences *'What's the point?'*	Using persuasive language, clear firm voice, fluent, rich warm middle-range tone, expresses all feelings including self-doubt and anger, not overloud or quiet, steady even pace, emphasis on key words, emphatic in making requests *'I think...'*

Table 9.4 Influencing styles characteristics (*Cont'd*)

	Aggressive	Adaptive	Apathetic	Assertive
	rises at end, abrupt, clipped, fast and fluent, uses critical or blaming words 'you must...' 'If you don't...' 'There is no alternative...' 'That's final' 'You must be kidding...' 'Never...'	'It's not really important...' 'Maybe you could only...' 'Well, perhaps we possibly might do a little...' 'Just a tiny thing...' 'Sorry...' Asking not telling	'If we really must...' 'Don't bother it's not worth it...' 'I'm not really much...' 'There's probably, um, somehow, nothing we can do...' 'I can't...'	'I feel...' 'I want...' 'How can we resolve this?' 'Let's...' *Telling* not asking
	Moving against	Moving away	Going nowhere	Moving towards

Most of us are unlikely to have one exclusive influencing style, but are more likely to have a mixture. Nevertheless, some participants may identify that they have one preferred style over the others. They may like to consider if their perception of their own style matches their colleagues' and customers' perceptions of them. They may also consider which style they believe to be most effective for dealing with challenging situations (as described in Chapter 8). They may also want to think about where they are currently in respect of influencing styles, and how this relates to where they would actually like to be. It may be useful to note this as it can be used later when action planning is discussed (Chapter 12).

Aim 2: To use assertive language in response to customer and staff statements

Assertiveness goals and skills

Broadly speaking, the goals of assertiveness are to:

- be confident in dealing with authority figures;
- be confident in trying out new ways of doing things and in taking 'risks';

- be less concerned with approval from others;
- be prepared and able to confront behaviour that you do not want or like;
- have greater confidence in making decisions;
- improve your self-concept and self-esteem;
- positively express your point of view.

To achieve these goals, the following key skills are important:

- admitting ignorance/asking for more information;
- asking for help;
- expressing your feelings;
- handling criticism from others;
- making a request/asking for what you want;
- offering compliments and appreciation;
- offering criticism to others;
- receiving compliments and appreciation;
- saying 'no'/refusing a request;
- speaking up for your own beliefs and values.

Each of these 'skills' can be handled aggressively or adaptively. The more they can be handled assertively, the greater the likelihood of personal effectiveness and satisfaction.

Transactional analysis

Transactional analysis (TA) is a way of understanding behaviour. It is based on the belief that we can learn from considering how our decisions and communications are based on our thoughts and feelings.

It uses the ego-state model (parent-adult-child) to help explain how people function and how they express their personality in their behaviour.

In the ego-state model, the *parent ego* is a state in which people behave/feel/think in subconscious mimicry of parental figures. It has two sides: the controlling parent and the nurturing parent. The former uses words/phrases like 'never', 'always' and 'why haven't you...?', while the latter uses phrases like 'oh dear', 'take care...', 'what a shame...' and 'I'll help you...'

The *adult ego* is a mature, deliberating element of personality in which actions are well-considered rather than the almost automatic responses of the parent ego. It involves asking questions and seeking out facts, e.g. 'why did this happen?', 'let us analyse the situation...', 'what are the options...', and 'how can this situation best be handled?'

The *child ego-state* has two facets. The first is the natural child – free, spontaneous and undisciplined. The latter is the adapted child, influenced by upbringing, which may result in compliance or rebellion. A member of staff receiving feedback on an appraisal may exhibit the child ego by responding rather sullenly to a critical assessment. Phrases employed in this state include 'I will in a moment...', 'I won't...', and 'If they can do it, then so can I...'

Life positions and the OK Corral

The philosophy of TA is that people are 'OK'. This means that everyone has validity and importance, and is deserving of equal respect. In TA theory, the term 'life positions' is used to refer to subconscious feelings about life that influence person-to-person transactions. Initially, four life positions are posited:

- I'm not OK, You're OK.
- I'm not OK, You're not OK.
- I'm OK, You're not OK.
- I'm OK, You're OK.

By communicating in a particular way, we can create pressure – or be pressurised by others – to communicate in a way that matches the style. For example, if we talk to our customers or colleagues in a controlling parental fashion, we may elicit child-like responses. What we really want to achieve in our transactions with customers and colleagues is adult-to adult-communication, i.e. I'm OK, You're OK.

Depending on your influencing style, you will find yourself in a different place in the OK Corral:

- *I'm not OK, you're OK (adaptive)*:
  - gets away from others;
  - typical feelings include inadequacy, guilt, hurt, shame, stupidity;
  - people who take this position are likely to be seen as being submissive, playing helpless, being servile, lacking in confidence, non-assertive, lacking sharpness and energy;
  - gives self a lot of negative strokes;
  - adapted child ego-state (doing what you're told, compliant);

- victim;
- lose/win.

- **I'm not OK, you're not OK (apathetic):**
    - gets nowhere with others;
    - typical feelings include despair, apathy, weakness, rejection;
    - people who take this position are likely to be seen as very negative, low in energy, unresponsive, contributing very little, lacking initiative, unlikely to take care or take much trouble, quick to accept defeat and give up;
    - gives self and others a lot of negative strokes;
    - adapted child ego-state (harbouring guilt feelings, shame);
    - victim;
    - lose/lose.

- **I'm OK, you're not OK (aggressive):**
    - gets rid of others;
    - typical feelings include self-righteousness, indignation, hostility, impatience;
    - people who take this position are likely to be seen as domineering, arrogant, prejudiced, patronising, rigid, judgmental, devaluing others, treating people as stupid or nuisances;
    - gives others a lot of negative and/or phoney positive strokes;
    - critical parent ego-state (controlling/restricting rather than nurturing);
    - rescuer/persecutor;
    - win/lose.

- **I'm OK, you're OK (assertive):**
    - gets on with others;
    - typical feelings include a sense of energy, confidence, contentment, appropriate emotions for the situation, trust;
    - people who take this position are likely to be seen as confident in themselves and others, responsive, action-oriented, rational, calm under pressure, flexible, creative, interested in others and in working to solve problems, prepared to see others' points of view;
    - gives a wide range of positive and negative strokes, as appropriate;
    - adult ego-state (mature, deliberating);

- not victim/rescuer/persecutor;
- win/win.

To deal successfully with others, we must first deal successfully with ourselves. If you deal with customers in an assertive manner, you should encounter a win-win situation as described in the OK Corral scenario where 'I'm OK, you're OK'. Sisselman's (2009) research into the social styles of customers deals with how these styles might affect their understanding and perception of the quality of a particular customer service situation, namely the reference interview. From her research, it would appear there is a correlation between librarians' awareness of people's social styles and the outcome of the reference interview, emphasising the importance of developing awareness.

Bopp and Smith define the reference interview as the 'conversation between a member of the library reference staff and a library user for the purpose of clarifying the user's needs and aiding the user in meeting those needs' (Bopp and Smith, 1995: 37).

The purpose of the reference interview is to satisfy the library customer's information need. The librarian can use a number of communication, active listening and questioning techniques (see Chapters 5 and 6) to help identify the customer's precise need. Use is made of non-verbal communication, mirroring, paraphrasing, asking open questions and checking for understanding (Nilsen 2005).

Kaczorowski and Pinto (2009) also mention the reference interview in their article on the role of personality in interpersonal communication. Participants who find the present chapter particularly interesting may wish to pursue these references.

Assertiveness techniques

Despite all our best intentions, in certain demanding situations we may still harbour feelings of under-confidence. In such circumstances, we can overcome these negative feelings by adopting certain, positive patterns of behaviour. By *doing* something positive, we can largely defeat that sense of *feeling* negative. We will now examine the behaviours and techniques that will help to project the assertive approach that is so central to achieving the desired 'I'm OK, you're OK' outcome in any customer service scenario. Remember your communication skills:

1. (a) Actively listen to what is being said then show the other person that you both hear and understand by responding positively and effectively.

   (b) If you are on the phone, you may find that standing up while having your conversation may help you sound more confident and in control.

   (c) Smiling can help you sound more confident too.

2. (a) Say what you think or feel. Be specific and direct. Use positive rather than negative language – e.g. 'I want...' not 'I don't want...'

   (b) Speak clearly, don't mutter.

   (c) It helps to stop on occasion and silently ask yourself 'What am I feeling now?' You don't have to take your feelings out on colleagues and customers. Sometimes just understanding your own feelings can help you recognise your own needs and hence feel more confident.

   (d) You can increase your proactive skills by using 'I feel...' statements (verbally and non-verbally) and help develop your ability to respond to, rather than react to customers and situations.

   (e) Focus and act on those things you can personally do something about. Stop worrying about things you can't.

3. (a) Maintain your position and do not allow yourself to be drawn into an argument or a defensive statement. Excuses, defensive statements and insults weaken your position. If necessary, repeat your statement or request calmly.

   (b) Don't join in with the perpetual 'moaners' or colleagues who are prone to bad-mouthing others. They can bring you down too. In protecting your own positive thoughts, you will also protect your self-esteem.

4. Say what you want to happen. Leaving things unsaid can block confidence and self-esteem. Clearing the air can be as good for you as clearing your desk – dealing with unfinished business makes you feel better.

Assertiveness quizzes

As an alternative or additional exercise to the rather lengthy influencing styles questionnaire, we offer some smaller quizzes (a mini-quiz and two midi-quizzes, if you will) that participants might like to complete use to assess their own assertiveness.

Mini-quiz

		Always	Often	Sometimes	Rarely	Never
1	I can ask for help from others					
2	I express emotions openly and directly					
3	I can say 'no' to the demands of others					
4	I complain in a shop if the service is poor					
5	I like to share my ideas with others					

Score as follows:

- Always: 4
- Often: 3
- Sometimes 2
- Rarely: 1
- Never: 0

Result:

- *Over 13*: You stand up for your rights.
- *8–13*: You could be more assertive.
- *Below 8*: You are a bit of a pushover.

Midi-quiz 1

		Often	Sometimes	Rarely	Never
1	I am able to speak with confidence in a difficult meeting where tempers running high				
2	If I am unsure of something I can easily ask for help				
3	If someone is being unfair and aggressive I can handle the situation confidently				

		Often	Sometimes	Rarely	Never
4	When someone is being sarcastic at my expense or at the expense of others I can speak up without getting angry				
5	If I am being put down or patronised I can raise the issue directly without being aggressive				
6	If I believe I am being taken for granted I am able to draw attention to it without sulking or getting upset				
7	If someone asks my permission to do something I would prefer them not to (e.g. smoke), I can say no without feeling guilty				
8	If someone asks my opinion about something, I feel quite comfortable giving it even if I think my opinion will be unpopular				
9	I can deal easily and effectively with senior staff				
10	When given faulty or substandard goods in shops and restaurants I can state my case well without attacking the other person				
11	When an important opportunity is in the offing I can speak up on my own behalf				
12	When I can see something going wrong I can draw attention to it early without waiting until it is a potential disaster				
13	When I have bad news to give I can do it calmly and without excessive worry				
14	If want something I can ask for it in a direct, straightforward way				
15	When someone isn't listening to what I am saying I can get my point across without becoming strident or feeling sorry for myself				

		Often	Sometimes	Rarely	Never
16	When someone misunderstands me I can point it out without feeling guilty or making the other person look small				
17	When I disagree with the majority view I can state my case without apologising or getting high-handed				
18	I take criticism well				
19	I give compliments without being embarrassed or it sounding like flattery				
20	When I get angry, I can express my point of view without becoming judgmental or feeling I have let myself down				
	Totals				

Adapted from Rennie Fritchie Consultancy.

Score as follows:

- Often: 1
- Sometimes: 2
- Rarely: 3
- Never: 4

Result:

- *50–80*: You need to do considerable work to develop assertive behaviour.
- *35–50*: Your assertive behaviour lacks consistency. You need to work to improve this.
- *25–35*: Although you can be assertive you would benefit further from self-development.
- *20–25*: You are confident and assertive in your approach to situations.

Midi-quiz 2

Look at each statement carefully. Consider how much you agree or disagree with the statement and put a tick in the box that best represents your view.

	I have the right to...	Strongly agree	Agree	Neither	Disagree	Strongly disagree
1	Be treated with respect as a thinking, feeling human being					
2	Set my own priorities					
3	Express my feelings, opinions, values					
4	Be heard when I wish to say something					
5	Require an explanation of other people's actions if they affect me					
6	Say I don't understand					
7	Say 'no' to other people's requests without explaining					
8	Insist that I get what I pay for					
9	Change my mind					
10	Make mistakes without feeling guilty and learn from them					
11	Ask for what I need or want					
12	Decline responsibility for the problems of others					
13	Deal with others without being dependent on them for approval					
14	Spend some time each day as I wish					
15	Have my own physical space on which no one may impinge					
	Totals					

Score by totalling the number of ticks in each column, then multiplying as follows:

- Strongly agree × 5
- Agree × 4
- Neither × 3
- Disagree × 2
- Strongly disagree × 1

Result:

- *15–30*: You need to do considerable work to develop assertive behaviour.
- *31–45*: Your assertive behaviour lacks consistency. You need to work to improve this.
- *46–59*: Although you can be assertive you would benefit further from self-development.
- *60–75*: You are confident and assertive in your approach to situations.

OK Corral scenarios

The following are some scenarios and accompanying statements that illustrate different life positions and communication methods. Some of these are fairly extreme and, we hope, unlikely to be encountered in real-life situations. When analysing the example scenarios and statements, participants may wish to start by referring back to their earlier work on influencing styles and where they place you in the OK Corral. More importantly, the exercise is designed to give participants an opportunity to get together in groups of say three, and to work out some suitably assertive responses to the example scenarios.

- Customer is trying to track down a subject specialist on a subject-related floor of the library.

  Customer: I don't seem able to find anyone to help me.

  Response: They are all in a meeting.

- Student customer is searching for textbooks related to a module or unit on the course he is undertaking.

  Customer: There are never any books on the shelves for my course

  Response: We don't have enough money to buy multiple copies.

- Member of academic staff has come to the technical services section to check on the progress of a book they are eagerly awaiting.

  Customer: I ordered this book three weeks ago. When will it arrive?

  Response: I haven't a clue.

- Member of the public, unfamiliar with the library, comes in to see if a book she would like to read is in stock.

  Customer: Do you have this title?

  Response: You will have to look it up on the OPAC for yourself.

- Customer has found that a recent issue of a journal has been vandalised.

  Customer: The article I need has been cut out of this magazine.

  Response: It is not us that tears out the pages. It is those blasted students.

- Student user of an academic library is trying to obtain photocopies larger than the conventional A4 size.

  Customer: Can this photocopier be changed so it copies A3 size documents?

  Response: We don't do that for students.

- Customer has been unsuccessful tracking down a book on the shelves.

  Customer: The catalogue says this book is not out on loan but I can't find it on the shelves.

  Response: Don't blame me.

- A customer is in the interlibrary loans section

  Customer: Could you get this book for me?

  Response: We will try to get it if you like.

- A customer finds that the printer associated with the computer on which he is working is not functioning.

  Customer: How long will it be before the printer is working?

  Response: I haven't a clue.

- Another customer has entered the interlibrary loans section.

  Customer: Can you get me this book in two days?

  Response: Don't be silly.

- A customer needs some technical assistance.

  Customer: Can you tell me where the technicians are?

  Response: No, I am not their keeper.

Further OK Corral scenarios

Here are some real-life scenarios that may be used to generate further discussion on how best to respond in an assertive manner. These have all actually happened either to the authors or to colleagues. We have refrained from detailing what our 'assertive' responses were....

- There is a mix-up in respect of appointments. A customer has arrived expecting to see a reference librarian about a fairly complex, subject-specific query and the member of staff in question already has a customer with him. A lengthy wait may be involved.

- The silent floor in the library forbids the use of mobile phones. There are prominent notices to this effect. While on that floor you hear a mobile phone ring and then the beginning of a conversation. The recipient of the call does not appear to be about to leave the building

- The only drinks allowed in the library are bottles of water. The only exception to this rule is in the seminar room where workshops are held and where there are no materials or equipment likely to be damaged by spillages. A customer comes into the building carrying what appears to be a closed can of soda.

- You are dealing with a customer at the counter. You have to leave the computer to check some files at the back of the service area. When you move away, the customer with whom you are dealing takes hold of your computer screen and turns it towards him, proceeding to look at the information thereon.

- It is rag week at the university and prices in the students' union bar are at rock-bottom. Two students on the floor of the building where you are working have removed some of their clothing and are taking photographs of each other.

- There is a vending machine in the library café area. It is an open day and several school groups are being shown around. Some unaccompanied children are now in the café area and appear to be fiddling with the machine.

- A slightly disreputable looking person, unfamiliar to you as a regular customer, is at the service desk on your floor. You are unsure if he is drunk, on drugs or just in high spirits, but he has started to serenade the member of staff sitting at this desk.

- In an inner-city public library, the local vagrants sometimes use the building for shelter, particularly during inclement weather. This is not usually a problem, but on this occasion, a member of the public advises you that they are leaving the building because there is a vagrant sitting in the reading room surrounded by magazines and newspapers, and his coat is covered in excrement. The member of the public strongly emphasises their concern that this represents a serious risk to health.

Further reading

Berne, E. (1973) *Games People Play: The Psychology of Human Relationships*, London: Penguin.

Berne, E. (1975) *What Do You Say After You Say Hello*, London: Corgi.

Board, R. de (1997) *Counselling for Toads: A Psychological Adventure*, London: Routledge.

Bopp, R. E. and Smith, L. C. (1995) *Reference and Information Services: An Introduction* (2nd edn), Englewood, CO: Libraries Unlimited.

Cranford, J. (2000) 'Public and reference services', *Arkansas Libraries* 57(3): 23–4.

Field, L. (2001) *60 Tips for Self-Esteem*, Shaftsbury: Element

Harris, A. B. and Harris, T.A. (1995) *Staying OK*, London: Arrow.

Harris, T. A. (1995) *I'm OK, You're OK* (new edn), London: Arrow.

James, M. and Jongeward, D. (1996) *Born to Win: Transactional Analysis with Gestalt Experiments* (4th rev edn), Cambridge MA: Perseus.

Kaczorowski, M. M. and Pinto, H. (2009) 'Getting personal: understanding personality types for better communication', *AALL Spectrum* 13(1): 18–19, 33.

Merrill, D. W. and Reid, R. H. (1999) *Personal Styles and Effective Performance: Make Your Style Work for You*, New York: CRC Press.

Nilsen, K. (2005) 'Virtual versus face-to-face reference: comparing users' perspectives on visits to physical and virtual reference desks in public and academic libraries', *World Library and Information Congress: 71st IFLA General Conference and Council*, Oslo, 14–18 August, available at: *http://archive.ifla.org/IV/ifla71/papers/027e-Nilsen.pdf* (accessed 30 January 2010).

Rees, S. and Graham, R. S. (1991) *Assertion Training: How to Be Who You Really Are*, London: Routledge

Sharp, D. (1975) *I'm OK, You're Not So Hot*, New York: Warner Paperback Library.

Sisselman, P. (2009) 'Exploiting the social style of patrons to improve their satisfaction with the reference interview', *Library Review* 58(2): 124–33.

The Solicitors' Coach Assertiveness Profile. Available at: *http://www.the solicitorscoach.co.uk/phdi/p1.nsf/pages/1801:AssertivenessProfile.pdf/$file/AssertivenessProfile.pdf* (accessed 23 October 2009).

Steiner, C. (1990) *Scripts People Live: Transactional Analysis of Life Scripts* (2nd edn), New York: Grove.

Stewart, I. and Joines, V. (1987) *TA Today: A New Introduction to Transactional Analysis*, Nottingham: Lifespace Publishing.

Woollams, S. and Brown, M. H. (1979) *TA: The Total Handbook of Transactional Analysis*, Englewood Cliffs, NJ: Prentice Hall.

10

Suggestions for improvement

I have not failed. I've just found 10,000 ways that won't work (Thomas Edison)

There's always room for improvement, you know – it's the biggest room in the house. (Louise Heath Leber, on being chosen Mother of the Year, 1961)

Aims

The aims of this chapter are as follows:

- to identify how participants can help improve the effectiveness of their section.
- to identify how managers can help participants make improvements.

To assist with planning, Table 10.1 presents a suggested session plan.

Background

Those of you with access to UK television may have seen a Channel 4 series in the summer of 2009 entitled *I'm Running Sainsbury's*. The programme acknowledged the fact that all staff, including shelf-stackers, cleaners, trolley-pushers and checkout assistants might have the next 'big idea' – after all, these staff are closest to the challenge of the business. In the programme, selected staff were given the opportunity to showcase their ideas to the senior management team and, in some cases, were empowered to drive their ideas.

Table 10.1 Session plan – suggestions for improvement

Session	Aims	Content	Methods	Aids	Time (mins)
Suggestions for improvement	To identify how participants can help improve the effectiveness of their section		T		5
		Looking from the outside in	A	F/C	15
	To identify how managers can help participants make improvements	Suggestion box	A	F/C P/I	20
		Our changing customers	A	F/C	15
		Customer feedback	A	H/O	15
Approx. total time (mins)					70

*A, activity (participants); F/C, flipchart; H/O, handout; P/I, Post-it notes; T, talk (facilitator)

This book is about customer care. How far do your staff care? For staff to care, they need to be trained and motivated. In addition, they need to know that their contribution is valued. One way to acknowledge their contribution is to afford them an opportunity to put forward suggestions for improvement.

As Seath says, 'All the "smile training" in the world won't make any difference to service quality if the basic service delivery systems aren't up to it, especially if no one is working to improve the systems' (Seath, 1992: 185).

Aim 1: To identify how participants can help improve the effectiveness of their section

Looking from the outside in

As people who manage services, we can sometimes become preoccupied with immediate operational and professional or technical issues.

For this activity, participants are invited to put themselves in the customer's shoes and to imagine that they are a library customer, e.g. a student or an academic member of staff.

Focusing on a specific service or activity, participants should imagine how they, as a customer, would answer the following questions. They should work on this individually, jotting down a few brief notes in response to the questions, and should be prepared to share them with the other participants.

The questions are as follows:

- What sort of 'image' would you say the department/section/service has?
- How easy is it to use the service?
  - Is access easy?
  - Is telephone access uncomplicated?
  - Are forms, notices and letters clear, simple and helpful?
  - Is the atmosphere friendly and welcoming?
  - How easy to use are the facilities and equipment?
- How much information are you given by the department/section/service about:
  - services available;
  - policies;
  - your rights;
  - the standards it is trying to achieve?
- How well do staff treat you?
  - Is the reception welcoming and cheerful?
  - Can they respond to you quickly?
  - Can they give you information or advice?
  - Can they make decisions?
- How efficient does the department/section/service seem?
  - Is it well organised; or
  - Bogged down in red tape?
- Are you ever asked what you want from the service or think about the service?
  - How is this done?
  - How often?
- What other comments (if any) would you make about the service?

After this individual exercise, the participants should form groups of three or four people. Where possible, the groups should comprise participants who work within the same department/section/service. Participants should share their perceptions about customers' views, noting positive comments and negative comments on a flipchart under those two headings.

Suggestion boxes

These activities should lead you nicely into the later section of this chapter which deals with feedback.

Option 1

In an ideal situation, groups of three or four participants from the same section/work teams should work together for this activity. If this isn't possible, facilitators may prefer to use one of the alternative versions of the exercise, as described below

Having divided a flipchart into two columns, participants are asked to add their section or team name as the heading for the first column. Below this, they should write a list of their suggestions on how to improve their section. In the second column, participants should write a note of the ways that managers could help them to achieve the improvements. After each group has presented its list, the whole group, along with the facilitators, should look at any common themes that may emerge.

Option 2

For this activity, participants are asked to complete the following four statements, bearing in mind that their targets must be SMART (specific, measurable, agreed, realistic and timed):

- My customer service skills are currently effective in the following areas:
- I need to improve my customer service skills in the following areas:
- My team/section could make my job easier if:
- To consistently exceed customers' expectations we need to change:

Ideas and suggestions from the different groups can be merged onto a flipchart to aid group discussion. During the exercise, the individual content can be checked out for intelligibility by asking participants:

- If you were not in this group, would you understand this?
- How can it be made clearer?

Post-it® notes or Genius Pads™ should be distributed to participants, who should split the task of writing one suggestion per note/pad. These can then be spread out on a table or the floor so participants can walk around and read them. Ask the participants to mark all the notes that deal with a particular topic (e.g. put 'IT' against all those dealing with technology; 'TRN' against those dealing with training etc.)

The notes will tend to cluster into categories, but with a certain degree of overlap.

As a whole group, participants should then consider the categories they have clustered and ask:

- Is this item actionable?
- Can we do anything about it?

If an item is not actionable and they can do nothing about it, perhaps it should be excluded. They should omit anything they are already doing or which is part of their programme

Participants should beware of items beginning 'More...' – it is seldom worth considering a bottomless wish list. Participants should consider the feasibility, the likely consequences and the risks related to the different suggestions.

Another approach to the above suggestion box activities is for the participants as a group to assess the suggestions and rank them as 'smoking', 'smouldering' or 'burning' issues, with 'burning' being deemed the most important and 'smoking' the least.

Participants or facilitators may wish to review what is produced after the completion of training and pass this on to the senior management team or similar – with the participants' agreement, of course.

Option 3

For this version of the activity, participants are asked to discuss how they might not only improve their customer service but also exceed customer expectations. This approach results in more general suggestions than the previous versions of activity but is more suitable where you do not have participants from the same sections/departments.

Table 10.2 presents suggestions derived from a session with a group of staff from a higher education establishment. The themes were identified by the facilitators after the event. If the participants are getting stuck, you might want to suggest some of these themes for them to consider.

Table 10.2 Improving customer service and exceeding customer expectations

Theme	We need to ...
Expectations	set clear expectations for ourselves and for our customers
	pre-empt customers' expectations and anticipate their needs
	be clearer about the service standards we must maintain or improve upon, e.g. produce a service level agreement or charter to help manage customer expectations; define the baseline of minimum service; establish key performance indicators (KPIs)
	reflect on our own expectations as customers; walk in their shoes
	try to personalise services and tailor them to individual customers and contexts; each customer is unique so service should be consistent but flexible
	pay attention to detail, 'put a cherry on the cake' – but might this raise future expectations which are then disappointed?
	try to develop relationships with customers
Practices and procedures	clarify our standards and practices
	review our practices and our documentation
	be more proactive with our policies and procedures
	stand back from each process and work out information and data-flow needs, e.g. ask stakeholders what is needed, when and why
	look at some of our more complex procedures in terms of user-friendliness and consider how we could improve them
	help customers to help themselves, e.g. take ownership of their own data or information requirements

Table 10.2 Improving customer service and exceeding customer expectations *(Cont'd)*

Theme	We need to ...
Staff attitudes	be prepared to share; build a shared knowledge base
	be prepared to ask for help and to help/support colleagues
	be willing to adapt and think creatively
	display a positive attitude, avoiding complacency and avoiding pessimism
	challenge and seek to change 'old school' attitudes of recidivists and poor customer service providers
	display efficient and professional attitudes
	present a united front, focusing on common goals and our roles in achieving them
	respect colleagues as well as customers
Networking & communication	improve internal relationships, establish shared priorities and clarify interdependence of working relationships
	meet colleagues outside work setting to help with bonding, teambuilding and understanding of roles
	meet customers regularly to identify their needs and to share information, proactively communicating with user groups
	make 'house calls' – get out the office a bit more instead of dashing off e-mails
	improve communications and knowledge sharing, networks across the organisation and cascading of information up, down and across
	share best practice with similar organisations in the area; document good service; pass on 'lessons learned'
Training	invest time in 'lessons learned' sessions – make these a part of the overall evaluation process, not one-off events
	train people not only for what they are doing but what they potentially can do
	have regular training slots, e.g. close for half an hour once a week for updates
Responsibility	take ownership of a query, ensuring the loop is closed; this satisfies customers and improves our knowledge base
	take responsibility for our 'bit' and for the wider process
	say what we can do rather than what we cannot
	be aware of appropriate points of referral
	acknowledge good service given by colleagues and share with the wider team

Table 10.2	Improving customer service and exceeding customer expectations (Cont'd)

Theme	We need to ...
	develop a culture of 'praise' but not so often that it becomes meaningless
	anticipate change – and its consequences
	pre-empt problems or 'opportunities'
	consider how we can give value-added
	evaluate and continuously improve
Feedback	examine how we follow up complaints/criticism
	deal with positive and negative feedback; learn how to give and receive constructive feedback and act upon it
	acquire feedback (e.g. questionnaires) and react accordingly
	consider how feedback is disseminated
	consider whether we have effective ways to solicit feedback

Our changing customers

This exercise forms a useful prelude to the final chapter and the activities included in it. Facilitators may wish to use this as a linking exercise. In this activity, the participants are asked to consider how their customers' expectations are changing (i.e. what do they expect) and, in conjunction with this, consider how effective current customer service is in meeting or exceeding such expectations.

The suggested approach for the facilitator(s) is to initiate a group discussion, and to use flipcharts or whiteboards to note down all valid suggestions offered by participants. To focus further discussion, it is useful to then categorise the suggestions into themes. These themes should ideally be identified by the participants themselves.

Tables 10.3 and 10.4 are based on a customer care session. The facilitators have identified some of the themes and, if your participants are struggling, you might want to suggest these as a starting point.

Table 10.3 Our changing customers

Theme	Changes
Concept of the customer	Customer base is changing
	There is no such thing as a typical customer
	Increasing diversity of customers and needs
Customer attitudes	Consumer culture, expectation of value for money
	More demanding customers
	Wider set of expectations
	Expectation of equity, consistency of service
	More proactive customers, user groups (comparing experiences)
	Clarity of requirements in terms of facilities, equipment, support
	More knowledgeable, with more specialised requests
Technology	Modern up-to-date environment
	Demand for 24/7 out-of-hours support – help lines etc
	No bedding-in period for systems – instant response, rapid solutions
	Demand for immediate response to e-mails
Customer demands of service	Loop to be closed when a request is made
	'Spoon feeding', making it difficult to balance with giving support
	Seamless service, a one-stop shop where at the first point of contact all the answers are in one place
	Clear communication
	Data accuracy
	Reliability
	Consistency
	Transparency
	Personalisation
	Quick turnaround time
Customer demands of staff	Respect
	Approachability
	Knowledge/expertise
	Positive attitude
	Proactivity
	Friendliness
	Professionalism
	Effective communication skills
	Responsive to the needs that customers articulate

Table 10.4 Effectiveness in meeting expectations

Theme	How are we doing?
Culture	Resistance to change*
	Sections/departments running as individual businesses, 'fiefdoms' and silo mentality
	Conflicting priorities
	Areas with a higher level of resource to meet customer expectations can create problems for areas with limited resources
	High staff turnover, impact on understanding complexity of roles/tasks
	Constantly changing environment, restructuring
	Succession planning
	Public image problem
	Working at changing the culture as well as customer expectations – which is impacting on which?
	Mixed messages on the service come down from senior colleagues which can make area feel undermined
How are we doing?	We are not complacent
	We are often not as good as we could be
	We try to be reactive and proactive
	We may commit inefficiencies
	We aim for consistency while respecting differences
	We efficiently respond to queries and requests according to response policies in place – but is this meeting customer expectations?
	Service is patchy
	It can be difficult to get responses from general enquiry services
	Service could be more holistic
	Service is very reliable on individual's attitude, training, support, skills and workload
Communications and knowledge sharing	Need to ensure good information flow between areas
	Important to gain and update knowledge of other areas and roles
	Over-reliance on informal networks

Table 10.4　Effectiveness in meeting expectations (*Cont'd*)

Theme	How are we doing?
Training and development	Constantly re-evaluating and enhancing
	Different training experiences for old vs new employees
	Needs to be a continuum of development and up-skilling
	Staff to be empowered
Technology	Improving use compensates for lack of resources and the impossibility of being 'present' to help with every customer query
	Out-of-hours support
	Interconnectivity of systems
	Customers empowered to solve their own problems with access to solutions procedures
	Systems failure can frustrate customers and result in lack of confidence in service
	Data auditing needs to ensure data accuracy
Feedback	Much feedback is anecdotal
	We try to be consultative, e.g. user groups
	In some areas there is feedback 'fatigue' – customers are being bombarded with surveys
	Surveys could be better designed
	Feedback mechanisms are patchy and used irregularly
	Some feedback is not current
	Some service delivery aspects are tangible and measurable so we could have indicators
	We could benchmark and share good practice
	Results of a recent survey indicate we are sustaining the highest possible level of service with the current resources available to us
	There is always room for improvement

*'Some libraries retain a bias that keeps attitudes stuck in the past, no matter how much reality changes' (Hyman, 1999: 54).

Aim 2: To identify how managers can help participants make improvements

When we talked in Chapter 4 about providing for customer needs, this should be seen against the background of the resources available to us in term of staff, money, time and materials. We therefore have to know our customers' wishes and expectations. The advantage of this user-oriented approach is that we can promote specific services to specific groups, and direct our product more effectively, efficiently and more cost-beneficially to the most receptive audience. Establishing customer needs means getting feedback from your customers about their experience of your existing services.

Quantitative data, i.e. facts and figures about your service are often available thanks to the technology. Systems can provide data about demographics, occupancy, transactions etc. Qualitative data, i.e. opinions and perceptions, can be more difficult to come by, but this is the very information that tells you most about your customers' expectations and needs.

Ideally, you need a mixture of quantitative and qualitative data gathered in different ways to cross-check your results. This use of multiple methods is known as triangulation.

There are many books written on research methods and these set out the advantages and disadvantages of different methods of collecting customer feedback – whether through interviews, focus groups or surveys, or telephone, the internet or e-mail – so we will not dwell on them here.

Library surveys/questionnaires can be valuable and informative, but they can also be expensive to administer, and many customers now feel survey fatigue because of the number of surveys to which they are subjected. There are several survey instruments available for libraries that do not wish to design their own, e.g. SERVQUAL, developed by Parasuraman et al. (1988), provides an outcome measure for managers to gauge their success. The Association of Research Libraries (ARL) partnered with Texas A&M University to develop, test and refine a modified version of the SERVQUAL instrument, resulting in LibQUAL+™, which benchmarks perceptions of library service quality (Kyrillidou, 2006). Using Google or a similar search engine, one can easily find numerous studies using the LibQUAL tool. If you are interested in exploring the concept of service quality, Hernon et al. (1999) discuss definitions and dimensions and cite some of the key literature on the topic. There are also instruments that measure specific aspects of service, e.g. the WOREP tool, which was developed in the mid-1980s for assessing in-person reference desk transactions (Paster et al., 2006).

In addition, there are tools that enable users to create, send and analyse their own web-based surveys, e.g. Fluidsurveys, Instantsurvey, Mysurveylab, Polldaddy, QuestionPro, Stellar Survey, Surveygizmo, Surveymonkey, Survs, Wufoo and Zoomerang. Hernon and Schwartz (2005) mention Surveymonkey and Zoomerang, and these two tools are also featured in comparisons (Balcomgroup, 2008; Listio, 2009). One library-based survey on the use of e-book readers using Zoomerang is the Olin Library Kindle Feedback Survey run by the Olin Library at Rollins College, Florida, USA (see *http://www.zoomerang.com/Survey/survey-intro.zgi?p=WEB2294WK39VMF*).

You may also get inspiration from articles describing other libraries' approaches, e.g. Jordan's (2005) paper on evaluating friendliness in a public library, which suggests questions to use and provides a simple methodology to adopt.

Focus groups afford an opportunity to collect people's views, but the recruitment of participants representative of the user population is notoriously problematic. Consider the categories you would wish to target, e.g. regular users, lapsed users and potential users. How could you get access to, and cooperation from, all these groups? As an alternative to a focus group, you may wish to conduct a workshop with stakeholders, such as those reported by McKnight (2007) for 'customer value discovery' research.

Mystery shoppers may be used to get a snapshot of the customer service situation, but these can be subjective and may lead to lack of trust among employees if they feel they are being 'spied' upon. Mystery shopping could be combined with customer journey mapping or a walk-through audit (Rowley, 1994), which tracks and describes the customer's experience as they encounter a set of services. The mystery shopper can record not only what happens to them, but also their response to the experience in order to identify ways of improving both staff/customer interaction and the customer experience (see the discussion of secret shopping in Chapter 6).

Managing expectations

Wehmeyer and Auchter (1996) describe the development of a customer service pledge at Wright State University Libraries, USA. Missingham (2001) lists the key components of the National Library of Australia service charter, which was developed through a process of internal consultation in 1998. Other examples are available on library websites, e.g. Wilhite and Beleu (2000)'s list of service standards that customers can expect from the reference services of seven federal depository libraries in the Oklahoma City area.

A service level agreement between the library and the customer can also to help manage customer expectations. Table 10.5 presents a sample service level agreement.

Table 10.5 A sample service level agreement

We will...	We would like you to...
Treat you with courtesy and respect	Treat our staff and other users with courtesy and respect
Ensure a pleasant, welcoming environment in which you can work	Respect the silent study areas Use specified areas for group work and discussions Not to disturb others with mobile phones or iPods
Ensure availability of appropriate resources	Treat our materials, property and equipment with care
Provide a friendly and helpful service responsive to your needs	Take care of your personal property and not leave valuables lying around
Be identifiable by our staff dress code (e.g. T-shirts)	Keep your library card safe and for your exclusive use – do not lend it to friends
Provide equity of access to services for all users	Not to tell anyone your computer user name or password Commit your login details to memory
Ensure our staff are trained to provide a quality service	Ask staff when you need help
Publicise the range of services offered to you	Check your e-mail regularly Check our website for notices
Keep you informed about regulations, opening hours etc. and any changes affecting these	Be aware of regulations as regards, opening hours, loan periods, fines, food and drink
Ensure equipment faults are dealt with as soon as possible once staff are informed about such problems	Inform staff of equipment faults
Take on board your comments and suggestions to help us improve our service	Tell us if you feel we are not fulfilling our obligations

Customer surveys

Be warned that, when customers expect to receive a customer satisfaction survey, they are likely to report less satisfaction with the service. Customers who do not realise they are going to be asked for their opinions are likely to report more satisfaction (Ofir and Simonson, 2001) so it is difficult to know how far ahead to publicise a forthcoming survey of this type.

Having suffered a poor response rate with our surveys, we decided to ask just one 'killer' question instead – a survey technique known as the 'One thing...' approach. Quite often, respondents say 'What, only one?' and actually provide multiple responses. Had they been presented with a two-page questionnaire they might not have been so keen to respond. We then put such statements on pre-paid postcards for external mail or provide in-house boxes in prominent places for internal mail.

Consider whether this approach would work for you. You might like to ask participants, based on their suggestions for improvements, to come up with one such question or statement. For example:

- One thing I like about PlateGlass Library is...

- One thing I dislike about Barkinghampstead Library is...

- One thing that the Burns-McCarthy Institute Library could do better is...

Your participants may well come up with some better ideas.

Customer evaluations of the quality of a service inevitably reflect on the performance of the staff providing the service. As a result of these evaluations, possible service improvements are identified and, if the resources are available, these may be implemented. To avoid inappropriate 'improvements', it is important to consider the enablers and barriers to change, as well as the attendant risks. As Ensinger and Grundy (2007) point out, major service changes/implementations should have accompanying justifying documentation. By recording and evaluating feedback received and actioned, a meaningful audit trail can be created and maintained.

You may wish to revisit your own suggestions for improvement at this stage and evaluate factors that would help or hinder the introduction of these suggestions before moving on to the next chapter.

Customer feedback

Prior to the sessions, the facilitators may wish to gather a selection of blank comments cards, surveys and questionnaires from restaurants, hotels, information centres and similar service organisations. These can be distributed to participants for them to critique. One can also find customer feedback forms online; these can be displayed onscreen if the technology is available, or – if you have time – printed out and distributed. As a starter, you might want to consider the following:

- Burnaby Public Library, BC: '2002 Burnaby Public Library survey' (*http://www.bpl.burnaby.bc.ca/user2002.pdf*)

- Hauppauge Public Library, NY: 'Hauppauge Public Library community survey' (*http://hauppauge.suffolk.lib.ny.us/pdf/survey.pdf*)

- Loveland Public Library, CO: 'Loveland Public Library Survey – Help us plan for the future' (*http://www.lrs.org/documents/comm_analysis/Lovelandsurv.pdf*)

- Rhode Island State Law Library: 'Rhode Island State Law Library User Survey 2003' (*http://www.courts.state.ri.us/library/RI_State_Law_Library_User_Survey_2003.pdf*)

- South Plainfield Public Library, NJ: 'South Plainfield Public Library Survey Questions' (*http://www.southplainfield.lib.nj.us/SURVEY QUESTIONS_2%5B1%5D.pdf*)

Finally, if you have no time or opportunity to do this, a sample survey is given below.

Typical pitfalls to consider include the following:

- We produced a two-sided A4 survey for postal distribution but failed to put 'PTO' or 'see over' on the bottom of the first page. In consequence, although respondents had to fold the survey to insert it into the prepaid envelope, several failed to complete the second side, rendering their input invalid.

- To make it easier for respondents, surveys frequently contain tick-box sections where respondents just check the box that matches, e.g. their age group:

  - under 21;
  - 21–25;
  - 25–30;
  - 31–35;
  - 35–40 etc.

  The problem here is knowing which box to tick if you are 25 or 35 years old. To avoid ambiguity, go for 'under 21', '21–25', '26–30', '31–35' etc.

- Assume that any statement you make can be misinterpreted. We had one survey where, after asking the customer for their nationality, we used the statement, 'I consider my country of origin to be…' We assumed this would clarify nationality where, for example, people were immigrants, refugees or asylum-seekers or perhaps first-generation citizens. However, several respondents completed this statement with the word 'developed'.

- Take care with double negatives, especially when using a Likert scale such as

  - strongly agree;

  - agree;

  - neutral;

  - disagree;

  - strongly disagree.

  The inclusion of a negative term such as 'not' or 'none' in a survey statement may cause confusion or ambiguity when applied to the scale.

- If you are surveying, e.g. within a university, and you wish to determine what students are studying, you can probably ask them for their college/faculty/school/department. If you start asking them for their course/module/unit you will probably end up with too many categories, making your results hard to analyse.

- Make sure you make your ranges equal, for example:

  For how many years have you been a member of the library:

  - less than one;

  - 1–5 years;

  - 5–15 years.

  In this example, by making the last range of years longer than the others, you are immediately weighting the results towards a specific answer (i.e. the last).

- Make sure you are not asking two questions in one, for example:

  What type of newspapers and magazines do you read:

  (a) local/national

  (b) international

  Local/national should be two separate categories.

- Don't ask questions that you think a respondent will not answer accurately, for example:

  How heavy is your workload in the library?

  - very low;

  - low;

- moderate;
- high;
- very high.

Realistically, is anyone going to admit to having a very low workload? Furthermore, the question 'How heavy...' tends to suggest a comparison, i.e. heavy compared with what?

Being able to look at a variety of comments cards, questionnaires etc. helps participants to decide what they like and dislike about survey elements, layouts, presentations, types of questions etc. Through such critiquing, they can learn some do's and don'ts about survey production. Consider what the survey results are likely to tell you about your customers' perceptions and needs. How will they help you to give better customer care and to exceed their expectations?

If there is sufficient notice about the training session, facilitators might ask each participant to bring along a questionnaire, survey, comments card etc. from somewhere other than their workplace. It is also worth asking participants to start looking out for such 'research' in their daily lives to become more aware of the good, the bad and the ugly.

The following handout from the fictional Greystone University Library provides a further example of a customer service feedback questionnaire. Once again, you may wish to invite participants to critique this either in pairs or as part of a group discussion.

Sample customer feedback form: Greystone University Library 24-hour service pilot

We are piloting all-day opening during the examinations period and would like to know what you think of the service, what facilities you are using and how the service has impacted on your academic work.

The questionnaire is anonymous. Please indicate your response by placing an X in the appropriate box or, where indicated, entering a written response.

1. *Which services did you use on your visit to GUL?*
   - I looked for books on the shelves;
   - I looked for journals on the shelves;
   - I used an electronic information source (e.g. CD-ROM, database, internet);
   - I used the library catalogue;

- I used printers/scanners/photocopiers;
- I checked out a book using the self-service machine;
- I checked in a book using the self-service machine;
- I reserved a book;
- I used the study space;
- I ordered an inter-library loan;
- other (please specify).

2. *How long did you stay in the library on your visit to GUL?*
   - less than one hour;
   - 1–4 hours;
   - more than four hours.

3. *How many times do you expect to use GUL over the 24-hour service pilot period?*
   - two or three times per week;
   - weekly;
   - less than once a week.

4. *How did you find out about the 24-hour service pilot?*
   - notice board/leaflet/plasma screen in GUL;
   - notice board/leaflet/plasma screen elsewhere on campus;
   - students' union;
   - GUL website;
   - from a member of faculty;
   - from another student;
   - other (please specify).

5. *How has the 24-hour service pilot benefited your studies?*

6. *Please add any comments or suggestions you have about extended service.*

7. *Are you:*
   - first-year;
   - second-year;
   - third-year;
   - fourth-year;
   - graduate student.

8. *To which department do you belong?*
   - Arts & Humanities;
   - Business Management;
   - Education, Psychology & Social Sciences;
   - Engineering & Technology;
   - Fine Art & Design;
   - Geography & Environmental Studies;
   - Law;
   - Medicine;
   - Physics & Chemistry;
   - Unsure.

9. *Are you*
   - full-time;
   - part-time;
   - distance learner.

10. *Are you*
   - UK resident;
   - international student.

Thank you for taking the time to fill in this questionnaire.

Please put the completed questionnaire into the suggestions box at the library exit.

Exemplar: Library Charter and Business Excellence Framework, Wollongong University

This particular quality and service excellence programme began at Wollongong in 2004, premised on the principles of business excellence as espoused in the Australian Quality Framework, now known as the Australian Business Excellence Framework. The application of these principles has led to transformational change, including significant improvements in client satisfaction.

Emphasis is placed on the quality audit approach, which focuses on identified critical success factors and agreed performance indicators, all related to service stakeholders, i.e. library customers, the university executive, library staff, suppliers and the community at large.

The challenges in accurately navigating such a framework are acknowledged, with particular focus on a subjective assessment of 'perceived value', which centres on the key performance indicator of customer and stakeholder satisfaction. Having carried out this assessment, the importance of regular benchmarking is emphasised – related both to internal measurement of success within the institution, and equally importantly, on measuring successful performance against that of other, perhaps competing organisations.

For further detailed information on this wide-ranging initiative, see: 'The Quality Journey' (*http://www.library.uow.edu.au/about/UOW026249.html*). The library's annual reports are also online (*http://www.library.uow.edu.au/about/UOW026372.html*), along with the results of recent surveys (*http://www.library.uow.edu.au/surveys/index .html*) and a description of the actions to which the library is committed in order to support continuous improvement.

Exemplar: Action Research, Bournemouth University Library

The rationale for this particular initiative was to try to move beyond flat satisfaction ratings via an accurate evaluation of the impact of library services. The required outcome was to give some structure to the future shape of library services, and to give a rationale for why one initiative may be preferred to another.

The first step was to take part in impact studies. The methodology was then rolled out to all schools within the university. Focus groups then continued, with separate target groups of researchers; including both staff and students. Further support was provided via triangulation from all measures of feedback – online, committees, informal discussions and observation.

Feedback has been consistently excellent – none better than in some externally conducted filming of a 'vox pop' exercise.

The library intends to continue with action research, reviewing feedback from all the different sources, including the blunt instruments of the National Student Survey, and occasional but targeted focus groups.

For further information, see Beard et al. (2007).

Further reading

Anonymous (2009) 'Customer service excellence at Dumfries and Galloway', *Information Scotland* 7(2): 5.

Balcomgroup (2008) 'Online survey site comparison – SurveyMonkey, SurveyGizmo and Zoomerang', available at: *http://www.thebalcomgroup.com/node/139* (accessed 30 September 2009).

Beard, J., Dale, P. and Hutchins, J. (2007) 'The impact of e-resources at Bournemouth University 2004/2006', *Performance Measurement and Metrics* 8(1): 7–17.

Begay, W., Lee, D. R., Martin, J. and Ray, M. (2004) 'Quantifying qualitative data: using LibQUAL+™ comments for library-wide planning activities at the University of Arizona', *Journal of Library Administration* 40 (3/4): 111–19.

Brochado, A. (2009) 'Comparing alternative instruments to measure service quality in higher education', *Quality Assurance in Education* 17(2): 174–90.

Brophy, P. (1995) 'Quality management in libraries', *Proceedings of the 1st Northumbria International Conference on Performance Measurement in Libraries and Information Services*, 31 August to 4 September, Newcastle upon Tyne: Information North, pp. 77–81.

Burnaby Public Library, BC (2002) 'Burnaby Public Library survey', available at: *http://www.bpl.burnaby.bc.ca/user2002.pdf* (accessed 1 October 2009).

Calvert, P. J. (1997) 'Measuring service quality: from theory into practice', *Australian Academic and Research Libraries* 28(3): 198–204.

Cook, S. (2004) *Measuring Customer Service Effectiveness*, Aldershot: Gower.

Davis, D. S. and Berstein, A. M. (1997) 'From survey to service: using patron input to improve customer satisfaction' *Technical Services Quarterly* 14(3): 47–62.

Ensinger, S. and Grundy, D. (2007) 'Charter mark can change your life', available at: *http://digitalcommons.bolton.ac.uk/libraryjournals/1* (accessed 26 September 2009).

EQUINOX, available at: *http://equinox.dcu.ie/reports/pilist.html* (accessed 30 September 2009).

Fluidsurveys, available at: *http://fluidsurveys.com/* (accessed 30 September 2009).

Hart, L. Gannon-Leary, P. and Noel, L. (1997) 'Use of focus groups in the evaluation of services', paper presented at the *2nd Northumbria International Conference on Performance Measurement in Libraries and Information Services*, 7–11 September, Newcastle.

Hauppauge Public Library, NY (2005) 'Hauppauge Public Library community survey', available at: *http://hauppauge.suffolk.lib.ny.us/pdf/survey.pdf* (accessed 1 October 2009).

Hernon, P. and Schwartz, C. (2005) 'Simplified data collection', *Library and Information Science Research* 27(1): 1–4.

Hernon, P., Nitecki, D. A. and Altman, E. (1999) 'Service quality and customer satisfaction: an assessment and future directions', *Journal of Academic Librarianship* 25(1): 9–17.

HM Government Cabinet Office (2008) *Customer Journey Mapping: A Guide for Practitioners*. London: Cabinet Office.

Hyman, K. (1999) 'Customer service and the rule of 1965', *American Libraries* 30(9): 54–7.

InstantSurvey, available at: *http://www.instantsurvey.com/* (accessed 30 September 2009).

Jordan, M. W. (2005) 'What is your library's friendliness factor?' *Public Library Quarterly* 24(4): 81–99.

Kyrillidou, M. (2006) 'LibQUAL+™: a project from StatsQUAL™', in: *Association of Research Libraries, 2006 Survey Results*, Washington DC: Association of Research Libraries, pp. 4–5.

LibQual, available at: *http://www.libqual.org/* (accessed 27 September 2009).

Listio for Web 2.0 (2009) 'Comparing Survey Applications: Zoomerang, SurveyMonkey, FluidSurveys, and MySurveyLab', available at: *http://www .listio.com/reviews/2009/01/comparing-survey-applications-zoomerang-surveymonkey-fluidsurveys-and-mysurveylab/* (accessed 30 September 2009).

Loveland Public Library (1999) 'Loveland Public Library survey – help us plan for the future', available at: *http://www.lrs.org/documents/comm_analysis/ Lovelandsurv.pdf* (accessed 1 October 2009).

Manjunatha, K. and Shivalingaiah, D. (2004) 'Customers' perception of service quality in libraries', *Annals of Library and Information Studies* 51(4): 145–51.

Marriott, J. W. and Brown, K.A. (1997) *The Spirit to Serve: Marriott's Way*, New York: Harper Collins.

McKnight, S. (2007) 'Acquisition and cataloguing processes: changes as a result of customer value discovery research', *Evidence Based Library and Information Practice* 2(4): 22–35.

Missingham, R. (2001) 'Customer services in the National Library of Australia: leading edge or dragging the chain?' *Australian Library Journal* 50(2): 147–55.

Morgan, D. L. and Krueger, R. A. (1998) *Focus Group Kit*, Vols 1–6, London: Sage Publications.

Mysurveylab, available at: *http://www.mysurveylab.com/* (accessed 30 September 2009).

Nitecki, D. A. (1997) 'Assessment of service quality in academic libraries: focus on the applicability of the SERVQUAL', *Proceedings of the 2nd Northumbria International Conference on Performance Measurement in Libraries and Information Services*, 7–11 September, Newcastle upon Tyne: Information North, pp. 181–96.

Ofir, C. and Simonson, I. (2001) 'In search of negative customer feedback: the effect of expecting to evaluate on satisfaction evaluations', *Journal of Marketing Research* 38: 170–82.

Olin Library, Rollins College (year unknown) 'Olin Library Kindle Feedback Survey', available at: *http://www.zoomerang.com/Survey/survey-intro.zgi? p=WEB2294WK39VMF* (accessed 1 October 2009).

Parasuraman, A., Zeithaml, V. A., and Berry, L. L. (1988) 'SERVQUAL: A multiple-item scale for measuring consumer perceptions of service', *Journal of Retailing* 64: 12–40.

Paster, A., Fescemyer, K., Henry, N., Hughes, J. and Smith, H. (2006) 'Assessing reference: using the Wisconsin-Ohio Reference Evaluation Program in an academic science library', *Issues in Science and Technology Librarianship*, No. 46, available at: *http://www.istl.org/06-spring/article2.html* (accessed 27 September 2009).

Peterson, R. M., Murphy, B., Holmgren, S. and Thibodeau, P. L. (2004) 'The LibQUAL+™ challenge: an academic medical center's perspective, Duke University', *Journal of Library Administration* 40 (3/4): 83–98.

Polldaddy, available at: *http://polldaddy.com/* (accessed 30 September 2009).

QuestionPro, available at: *http://www.questionpro.com/* (accessed 30 September 2009).

Rhode Island State Law Library (2003) 'Rhode Island State Law Library user survey 2003', available at: *http://www.courts.state.ri.us/library/RI_State_Law_Library_User_Survey_2003.pdf* (accessed 1 October 2009).

Rowley, J. (1994) 'Customer experience of libraries', *Library Review* 43 (6): 7–17.

Saunders, E. S. (2008) 'Meeting academic needs for information: a customer service approach', *portal: Libraries and the Academy* 8(4): 357–71.

SCONUL/LIRG (year unknown) 'Impact Initiative', available at: *http://www.sconul.ac.uk/groups/ performance_improvement/impact2.html* (accessed 30 January 2010)

Seath, I. (1992) 'Training – a waste of effort?' *Managing Service Quality* 2(4): 185–7.

South Plainfield Public Library (year unknown) 'South Plainfield Public Library survey questions', available at: *http://www.southplainfield.lib.nj.us/SURVEY QUESTIONS_2%5B1%5D.pdf* (accessed 1 October 2009).

Stellar Survey, available at: *http://www.stellarsurvey.com/* (accessed 30 September 2009).

Surveygizmo, available at: *http://www.surveygizmo.com/* (accessed 30 September 2009).

Surveymonkey, available at: *http://www.surveymonkey.com* (accessed 30 September 2009).

Survs, available at: *http://www.survscom/* (accessed 30 September 2009).

Thompson, B., Kyrillidou, M. and Cook, C. C. (2007) 'Library users' service expectations: A LIBQUAL™ study of the range of what users will tolerate', paper presented at the 7th Northumbria International Conference on Performance Measurement in Libraries and Information Services, 13–16 August, Stellenbosch.

Wehmeyer, S. and Auchte, D. (1996) 'Saying what we will do, and doing what we say', *Journal of Academic Librarianship* 22(3): 173–80.

Wilhite, J. and Beleu, S. (2000) 'Metrodocs reference service standards', available at: *http://www.odl.state.ok.us/usinfo/metrodocs.htm* (accessed 28 September 2009).

WOREP, available at: *http://worep.library.kent.edu/* (accessed 27 September 2009).

Wufoo, available at: *http://wufoo.com/* (accessed 30 September 2009).

Yeo, R. K. and College of Industrial Management (2009) 'Service quality ideals in a competitive tertiary environment', *International Journal of Educational Research* 48: 62–76.

Yu, M. L., Hamid, S., Taha, M. and Soo, H. P. (2009) 'The e-balanced scorecard (E-BSC) for measuring academic staff performance excellence', *Higher Education* 57: 813–8.

Zeithaml, V. A., Parasuraman, A. and Berry, L. L. (1990) *Delivering Quality Service: Balancing Customer Perceptions and Expectations*. New York: Free Press.

Zemke, R. and Schaaf, D. (1989) *The Service Edge*, New York: New English Library.

Zoomerang, available at: *http://www.zoomerang.com/* (accessed 30 September 2009).

11

Teambuilding

He makes things easier for himself who makes things easier for others. (Asian idiom)

It is amazing what you can accomplish if you do not care who gets the credit. (Harry S. Truman)

Teams have the potential to thrive more on the differences between members than the similarities (Peter Honey)

Aims

The aims of this chapter are as follows:

- to foster team spirit;
- to help understand how we work in groups.

To assist with planning, Table 11.1 presents a suggested session plan..

Background

We could not do our job without one another. Trust between colleagues and a feeling of interconnectedness can help forge us into a cohesive unit or team. We are brought together in a work situation and tend to meld together because we share operational values. In sharing such values, we are able to communicate well, to negotiate with each other without conflict or, if conflict occurs, to resolve it amicably. We are able to be mutually supportive, to rely on each other, and to be mutually accountable for our actions. We have already discussed being courteous and considerate to our customers. Our colleagues are our internal

Table 11.1   Session plan – teambuilding

Session	Aims	Content	Methods	Aids	Time (mins)
Teambuilding	To foster team spirit		T		5
		Teambuilding enablers and inhibitors	A		5
	To help understand how we work in groups				
		The Grey Mare's tale	A		30
		Jungle survival*	A		55
Approx. total time (mins)					40

*Add 55 minutes to this session if undertaking the jungle survival activity
*A, activity (participants); F/C, flipchart; H/O, handout; P/I, Post-it notes; T, talk (facilitator)

customers and our fellow team members are especially close colleagues, so we should treat them with courtesy and consideration. With respect to communication, also discussed earlier, we need to employ our listening skills and allow team members to express themselves without interruption in a way that affords every team member the opportunity to be heard.

The benefits of working as a successful team and the concomitant collaborative expertise can be substantial, but such effective relationships are not easy to achieve. We have probably all heard of the 'forming, storming, norming and performing' phases of team development, first developed by Tuckman (1965). To summarise:

- *forming*: getting together, exploring each other's behaviour, keeping feelings in check;
- *storming*: testing each other, seeing how much we can get away with, power play;
- *norming*: settling down, focusing on shared aims and developing a sense of common purpose;
- *performing*: achieving goals, working positively to resolve any conflict that does arise.

Some difficulties are inevitable, but by overcoming these, we are in a better position to realise the opportunities that crop up.

Humans are basically social beings. We need to interact with each other in order to meet our individual and group needs. While the ability to work independently is a valuable skill, more can be achieved and tasks can be enhanced through working interactively with others. A simple way to prove this can be to conduct a 'pub quiz' of about 20 general knowledge or Trivial Pursuit type questions. The first time around, get participants to answer these individually on a notepad. Then divide the group into teams and invite them to work together and discuss their answers, writing their final responses in a second column on their notepad. If you then compare individual scores versus team scores, you should find that team synergy has made the score in the second column greater than that in the first, thanks to the diverse knowledge and experience of the group members.

Aim 1: To foster team spirit

Teambuilding enablers and inhibitors

As an opening activity, we suggest asking the participants to consider what factors either enable or drive teambuilding and to freely exchange ideas for two minutes. Participants can then shout out these ideas from the floor, and the facilitator(s) can write them down on a flipchart or whiteboard. After this, the facilitator(s) can turn the question around and ask the participants to spend a further two minutes considering factors that inhibit teambuilding. These responses may also be recorded on a flipchart or whiteboard.

Table 11.2 presents enablers/drivers and inhibitors/barriers to teambuilding. This list was derived from a group exercise, but your participants may come up with different answers. The main thing is that participants start recognising enablers and barriers, and become more sensitised to the behaviour types that are undesirable in team members.

This chapter features two teambuilding exercises: the Grey Mare's tale and jungle survival. Depending on the needs of your participants and on the size of your group, you may wish to play one or both. The Grey Mare's tale is more suited to smaller groups, while the jungle survival exercise will work better with a larger group.

| Table 11.2 | Teambuilding factors |

Enablers/drivers	Inhibitors/barriers
Good communications, openness	Unwillingness to share information, fear of loss of control
Shared perceptions and expectations, sense of purpose, vision and commitment	Hidden agendas, 'what is in this for me?', self-interest, self-aggrandisement
Clarity and understanding about roles	Lack of clarity about roles, stereotyping team members and their roles, inequity in involvement, unequal contributions
Shared sense of humour, goodwill	Lack of trust in the team or members
Willingness to participate	Lack of respect for other team members
Enthusiasm for task in hand, prospect of shared success	Cynicism
Creativity and innovative thinking, involving suspension of assumptions	'We have always done it this way...' attitude – 'dinosaurs'
Delivering what was promised	Promising more than can be delivered
Good time management	Tardiness
Recognising the achievements of the team and of individual members	Lack of cooperation, with tensions and conflicts
Ability to compromise in the common interest, to be flexible	Stubbornness, resistance, defensiveness, refusal to budge over some issues

Aim 2: To help understand how we work in groups

Comments on the activities

These are two very different activities, but the common thread is to get people to think about what is needed for successful teamwork. In past iterations of these exercises, participants have come up with some of the following suggestions:

- clarity and sense of purpose;
- commitment;
- common goals;

- creativity;
- diversity of team membership;
- energy;
- equality – everyone has the right to speak and be heard;
- flexibility;
- good communications;
- it helps if it is fun;
- mutual needs;
- mutual respect;
- mutual support;
- mutual trust;
- organisational support;
- resources;
- shared ownership;
- shared values;
- shared vision;
- time to go through the whole forming, storming (etc.) process.

The Grey Mare's tale

This exercise might be described as a variant of Cluedo, insomuch as the participants are trying to solve an imaginary murder. The exercise can be played as a board game using any game board with a numerical grid. You will need dice, a dice-shaker or eggcup, and coloured counters, buttons or small toys to move around the board.

The exercise is over when the participants have identified:

- the time of the murder:
- the place where the murder occurred:
- the murder weapon:
- the murderer:
- the murderer's motive:

The clues (given below) need to be prepared in advance. If you are going to run several sessions then it is worth copying them onto thin cardboard so you can reuse them. On the reverse of each card, write the clue number in large letters in the top left-hand corner. Participants take turns to throw the die and move their counter the appropriate number of squares. They may then pick up the clue represented by the number on the square on which they have landed. If two players land on the same square, the second player may double the number on the square and pick up the clue for the doubled number. So, for example, if two players land their counter on the square numbered 5, the second player can pick up clue number 10. Participants will gradually pick up a variety of clues and can share the information that the clues convey to them. Ideally, the players will eventually have all the clues and will be able to solve the mystery.

If the game is played on a snakes and ladders board, you might want to have players collecting a clue if they climb a ladder, and forfeiting a clue if they go down a snake. For this version of the game, participants should be forbidden from taking notes so that they have to remember any clues they have forfeited. There are many potential variations that you might adopt – we are sure that you can think of more.

At the end of the exercise, facilitators should get the participants to consider how they performed as a team member. They should ask themselves the following questions:

- Did I let other team members participate?

- Did I dominate the exercise?

- Did I share information?

- Was I an active or passive participant?

- Was my contribution listened to?

- Was my contribution not enough/just right/too much?

On the basis of this exercise, the participants should also consider what helped and what hindered the team/group to work effectively. Their responses should recall some of the teambuilding factors in Table 11.1. Note that we advise self-assessment rather than peer assessment. Reflection is an important skill, and this exercise is not a competition to find the best team member!

The clues

1. When he was discovered dead, Mr Moffat had a large bruise and bleeding to the side of his head and deep cuts to his throat and neck.

2. Mr Hogg attacked Mr Moffat at 10.10 pm in the car park of the Grey Mare public house.

3. A man getting off the number 66 bus outside the Grey Mare saw Mr Moffat with blood all over his face.

4. A broken bottle with blood on it was found in the Grey Mare car park.

5. Mr Moffat's body was found at 11.15 pm.

6. When the man getting off the bus saw Mr Moffat he was sitting on the car-park wall, holding his head.

7. A spanner with Mr Moffat's blood on it was found in a dustbin near the Grey Mare.

8. Mr Hogg saw Mr Moffat in the bar and started threatening him.

9. Mr Moffat was having an affair with Mr Hogg's wife.

10. The barman saw Mr Selkirk leave the bar at 10.10 pm.

11. At 10.00 pm, Mr Hogg came into the bar and ordered a bottle of stout.

12. The spanner had Mr Selkirk's fingerprints on it.

13. Mr Hogg and Mr Moffat left the bar arguing at 10.05 pm.

14. The barman said that Mr Moffat and Mr Selkirk were regular customers in the Grey Mare.

15. The Grey Mare closed at 11.00 pm.

16. Mr Selkirk had been drinking on his own in the Grey Mare.

17. Mr Moffat's body was found in the back alley behind the Grey Mare.

18. The broken bottle had Mr Hogg's fingerprints on it.

19. Mr Moffat had been dead for one hour, according to a medical expert working with the police.

20. A regular customer going into the Grey Mare spotted Mr Selkirk opening the boot of his car in the Grey Mare car park just after 10.10 pm.

21. The barmaid found Mr Moffat very attractive.

22. Mr Moffat's bloodstains were found in the car park and back alley.

23. Mr Hogg had told Mr Moffat he was going to kill him.

24. The barman said that Mr Selkirk sometimes handed an envelope across the table to Mr Moffat.

25. Mr Moffat and Mr Selkirk met together from time to time in the Grey Mare.

26. Mr Selkirk could not be found by the police after the killing.

27. The number 66 bus stopped outside the Grey Mare at 10.12 pm.

28. It was obvious that the body had been dragged some distance.

29. Mr Hogg was not at home when the police called to make enquiries after finding the body.

30. The barmaid was off-duty on the night of the murder.

The answers

Mr Moffat had been involved in a fight with Mr Hogg in the Grey Mare car park because of Moffat's affair with Hogg's wife. Hogg had cut Moffat's face and neck with a broken bottle at 10.10 pm.

Moffat met Selkirk regularly in the pub. Moffat was blackmailing Selkirk. Selkirk saw his chance and clubbed Moffat to death with a spanner taken from his car at 10.15 pm. He dragged the body across the car park to the back alley and put the spanner in the dustbin.

In summary:

- time of the murder: 10.15 pm
- place where the murder occurred: the Grey Mare car park
- murder weapon: spanner
- murderer: Mr Selkirk
- murderer's motive: blackmail

Most participants manage to solve the mystery.

Jungle survival

Sometimes we just can't see the wood for the trees. For this reason, by distancing ourselves from our real-life situation, the long-range perspective can sometimes actually bring things into sharper focus. This exercise provides the opportunity to do just that – to step outside our daily routine, to assimilate a set of unfamiliar, exotic and challenging circumstances, and if we so wish, even adopt a totally different persona. By getting well outside our personal comfort zones – if only in our imaginations – we may well experience new perspectives, providing an opportunity for new insights into the interpersonal dynamics and the team-based processes that drive our daily working lives.

The group discussions triggered by this challenge can usually be directly related to situations we experience in our daily working lives. In basic terms, the core message of the exercise is to emphasise the fact that even a diverse group of people working together towards an agreed, common aim – in this case, survival – will be more successful than an isolated individual who is thinking and working alone, and is thus totally dependent upon their own, limited self-sufficiency. The message is that 'synergy works'.

This exercise aims to:

- explore group and individual dynamics in decision making; and
- emphasise the importance of synergy in achieving a positive outcome.

There is no peer rating or peer assessment in this exercise. The approach should focus on self-awareness, and on individual and team learning opportunities.

Preparing the exercise

The exercise should take no more than an hour, including initial briefing, the exercise itself, and debriefing.

Participants should divide into groups of ideally 5–12 people. Subdivide larger groups to try to achieve this optimum team size. Arrange tables and chairs to promote co-working, e.g. 'cabaret style'.

Give each participant two copies of the jungle survival information worksheet. Give each team a copy of the jungle survival team worksheet and a flipchart and a selection of marker pens.

Initial briefing – 10 minutes

- Explain that the group is about to take part in a group decision-making exercise. The scenario will be described in a verbal briefing, during which there will be no need to make notes, as individual and team handouts and worksheets will be circulated containing full details.

- Read out the individual briefing.

- Explain that when the individual worksheets are circulated, each group member should initially work separately on these, for a maximum of 10 minutes.

- Explain that the group will then be given a team worksheet, and will have a maximum of 20 minutes to achieve consensus on the allocated task. When the 20 minutes is up, the group will then compare its solution with the 'preferred solution' arrived at by survival experts.

- Explain that by way of conclusion, there will be a 15-minute discussion at the end of the exercise, during which participants will have the opportunity to reflect on any lessons learned as regards group decision-making, and on their relevance to their everyday work.

- Ask if there are any questions.

Running the exercise

- Circulate the individual briefing sheets and start the individual work session.

- After 10 minutes, close the individual work session, circulate the team briefing sheet and start the group exercise.

- After a further 20 minutes, close the group exercise, and discuss the preferred solution.

Individual briefing

You are an uninjured survivor from a small, passenger aircraft which was forced to crash-land in a clearing in isolated, remote jungle terrain. Neither the pilot nor the co-pilot survived the crash, and the flight had no cabin crew. Of your fellow survivors, only one is seriously injured, with two broken legs, although some of the other passengers have minor cuts and bruises.

Due to the sudden nature of the emergency, you know that your pilot was unable to transmit an emergency 'mayday' message before the crash. As such, the authorities as yet have no knowledge of either your predicament or your location. As regards location, all you know is that you are certainly several hundred miles from the nearest habitation. It will be dark within two hours.

You managed to recover 15 items from the aircraft before it burst into flames, destroying everything onboard. These items are as follows:

- 12 high-visibility inflatable lifejackets, each with a whistle;
- 400 cigarettes and six disposable lighters;
- 50 litres of fresh water, in one-litre plastic bottles;
- a one-litre bottle each of whisky, gin, brandy and vodka (no mixers!);
- a toilet bag, containing one bar of soap, one toothbrush, one tube of toothpaste, 12 plastic safety razors and one deodorant stick;
- an emergency map of the Amazon jungle, unmarked;
- one aircraft first-aid kit;

- one battery-powered transistor radio;
- one emergency axe;
- one pack (12 rolls) of luxury, soft white toilet paper;
- one standby emergency compass, removed from the cockpit;
- six bottles of insect repellent;
- three torches (flashlights) with batteries;
- two boxes of 50 muesli bars, two boxes of 20 chocolate bars, and 100 small packets of salted peanuts;
- two unopened parachute packs.

Your task is to rank these in order of their importance to your survival. Place the number 1 by the most important item, 2 by the second, and so on down to number 15.

Group briefing

Each of you will already have produced an individual priority listing. What you need to do now is to achieve group agreement on each of the items in the list. This may not be easy, as individual team members will doubtless have differing views on relative priorities. This is an exercise in achieving consensus agreement.

Aim to achieve at least partial mutual agreement on each item in the list. If you approach the exercise based on the following guidelines, you will improve your chances of consensus:

- Focus on the logical argument for determining relative priority. By all means, use your own individual judgment as a start point, but be prepared to be swayed by convincing, logical alternatives.

- Always be open to the opinions of others. Don't get 'stuck on transmit'. Remember to 'switch to receive' too. See differences of opinion as an opportunity to explore new possibilities, rather than just as something negative.

- Support only those arguments with which you are at least in partial agreement. Don't 'fall in line' simply to keep the peace, or for the sake of convenience. Stick to your 'logical guns'.

- Above all, don't adopt 'easy out' techniques such as 'majority vote', 'horse-trading' or 'averaging out'. This is intended to be an exercise in reasoned debate, leading to consensus agreement. Please don't reduce it to a mere exercise in mathematics!

The preferred solution

The armed forces are the acknowledged experts in survival techniques. Many detailed training manuals have been produced on the subject, dealing with survival in both peacetime and wartime scenarios, and covering every conceivable theatre of operations, from arctic to desert – and everything in between.

Regardless of the specific scenario, it is generally agreed that the four key areas to be addressed, in order of priority, are as follows:

- protection;
- location;
- water;
- food.

In the particular situation described here, the accepted wisdom is to stay with the aircraft wreck. In such circumstances, experience has shown that most rescues take place within about 36 hours of the incident.

As for the four key areas:

- *Protection*: Deal with our most immediate physical (and emotional) requirements in order to establish the best possible survival environment. Safety and shelter feature here.

- *Location*: Not just 'where are we?' – as we may have no idea, but more importantly, what can we do to highlight our location to those who may be searching for us.

- *Water*: In any survival situation, water is far more important than food. Even in a temperate climate, with no water supply we may die from thirst within three days or so. Depending on our own bodily reserves of fat, we may survive without food for approximately three weeks or more.

- *Food*: See 'water' above.

With the above in mind, the order of priority of the preferred solution is as follows:

1. *First-aid kit (protection)*: One of your team is seriously injured, and this must be treated as first priority. Others may also need attention for minor injuries. You want *everyone* to survive.

2. *Two parachutes (protection)*: With darkness falling within a couple of hours, these can be used to provide shelter in the form of a para-tepee

or wigwam. You could even cut one up, as three segments can be used as an effective, surprisingly comfortable, para-hammock slung between two trees. With two full-size 'chutes, you will not be short of parachute cord, and if you're wondering how to cut it – use the scissors you found in the first aid kit.

3. *One emergency axe (protection)*: This will be invaluable in constructing your para-tepee, and anything else you may wish to lash together with the many metres of parachute cord you have at your disposal. You can also cut wood for that all-important camp fire, which you will light with...

4. *Six disposable lighters (protection)*: With night falling, a reassuring camp fire can work wonders for morale. (Location also features here, as the fire may be seen from the air at night, and can also be used to create smoke for the benefit of daytime searchers). As for all those cigarettes, the smokers may also argue that their habit will serve as a deterrent to insects. Sadly for the non-smokers, they are actually correct in this instance. Nevertheless, I would prefer to rely on...

5. *Six bottles of insect repellent (protection)*: Worth their weight in a jungle setting – particularly after sundown...

6. *Three torches/flashlights (protection)*: It will be dark in two hours' time.

7. *Twelve high-visibility inflatable lifejackets (location)*: You are in a clearing in the jungle, and 12 highly visible, inflated lifejackets can be used as an effective marker to be seen from the air. Remove the whistles from each jacket and give them to team members for use if they become separated, or to guide land-based search teams.

8. *One pack (12 rolls) of luxury, soft white toilet paper (location – yes: location!)*: You are in a jungle clearing. In still air conditions, you can use some of this paper to produce an impressively large SOS or even a simple 'X' on the ground to be viewed by searchers from the air. Even if your sign is partially trashed by high winds, the remnants may still be sufficiently visible from the air to attract further interest.

9. *Fifty litres of fresh water (water)*: Having addressed the more immediate 'protection' and 'location' issues, you should now ensure that team members remain sufficiently hydrated. In situations such as this, the general guide is to drink sufficient to assuage thirst. There may well be other nearby water sources, but until you know this for sure, take care of what you have.

10. *Two boxes of 50 muesli bars, two boxes of 20 chocolate bars, plus 100 packets of salted peanuts (food)*: Time for supper. Not exactly cordon bleu, but enjoy, nevertheless. Even snacks such as these can provide a significant boost to morale. Note that salted peanuts may make you thirsty…

11. *The one-litre bottles of whisky, gin, brandy and vodka (not categorised)*: Although, based on its calorific value, the alcohol could conceivably be considered as 'food', it is certainly not in the same category as 'water'. In fact, the intake of alcohol – particularly in the form of neat spirits – actually has a dehydrating effect on the body. You could use it as a mild disinfectant, although at only 40 per cent proof it is hardly surgical spirit. Depending upon your particular persuasion, perhaps have a morale-boosting nightcap when you turn in, or you may wish to save it to crack open when you first sight the rescue helicopters.

12. *One toilet bag, containing soap, aftershave, a toothbrush, toothpaste, deodorant, and 12 plastic safety razors (unclassified)*: Not much practical use as a 'team' resource – although the deodorant and aftershave may be attractive after a couple of days in the jungle. Even the blades in the plastic safety razors are difficult to use for anything other than attacking the facial stubble.

13. *One transistor radio (unclassified)*: This is a receiver – not a transmitter, and even if you can pick up a signal, it is unlikely to be in your own language. You are certainly out of range of anything familiar.

14. *Standby compass (unclassified)*: The accepted wisdom in your current predicament is to stay put and await rescue. Quite apart from that, you have no idea where you are or which direction you should travel. This item is of no practical use.

15. *Emergency maps of the Amazon jungle (unclassified)*: Again, you have no idea where you are, and no one said that you were in the Amazon jungle in the first place. This item is of no practical use, other than as kindling for your first fire.

This 'preferred solution' is not set in concrete, and there is room for some minor variation. Nevertheless, what should be emphasised is that the first ten items are firmly within the protection, location, water and food list of criticality. Items 11 to 15 are not.

The facilitator should avoid getting into long justifications of relative priority if challenged, and should simply repeat that the preferred listing reflects an 'expert' view.

Remember that the purpose of this exercise is not to arrive at the 'correct' answer. It is to demonstrate the processes leading to effective group decision-making and the achievement of consensus.

Exemplar: Elmwood College of Further Education, Fife – teamwork in action

As reported by Barclay (2009), Elmwood College is a relatively small institution, which, like many others, has had to face up to the challenge of limited funding and resources in recent years. Recognising that its library accommodation no longer catered for the wide variety of learning styles of its current student population, the college approached the challenge in a positive manner, and what followed was so successful that it led to the institution being 'highly commended' in Scotland's Colleges Annual Awards.

A key element in the college's success has been the strong, productive relationships between the curriculum teams and the library staff. One of the library staff completed an MSc in which customer service in further education libraries was compared with that found in the retail sector. Although the research showed that many of the library customers' service expectations were being met, there was still room for improvement in certain areas. Following a comprehensive local survey of customer service needs, three key initiatives were identified:

- library staff were made more accessible to students, via a positive decision to introduce programmed 'rovering', where staff actually left their desks and co-located themselves with customers in order to provide immediate assistance if required;
- staff actively followed-up whether the initial response to a query had been successful, by returning to the customer a few minutes later to establish if further assistance was required;
- staff consciously focused on providing courteous service at all times, in which the customer felt both valued and respected – a key but often overlooked aspect of customer service.

Based on these three key initiatives, library staff fostered strong working relationships with student groups. The high measure of success that was achieved became evident in the next annual library survey. Another positive outcome was the ability to identify that some student groups had not been able to maximise the benefits of their library induction. In addressing this, library staff arranged for a group of 'hospitality students' to become directly involved in the induction process. As part of this process, a competition was set up to encourage and guide inductees in accessing a variety of library resources. An additional advantage of the exercise was that library staff could identify those students who were still experiencing difficulties. This information was fed back to their tutors, who were then able to develop individual learning plans for them, and to ensure that they had appropriate support. This positive approach to teamwork paid dividends, in that not only were the students' needs at the forefront, but both library and curriculum staff derived significant benefit from seeing their joint efforts deliver something worthwhile. Moreover, the 'hospitality' students also felt very much involved in this team effort.

In a separate but related initiative, it was recognised that the HNC healthcare group, consisting mainly of female students, only visited the college occasionally to contact their tutor. Home study was very much the norm, and this unsatisfactory situation had generated some student retention issues with the previous academic year's group. The challenge was to identify a customer support model to positively support these students. The preferred solution was to digitise some key texts – having obtained the appropriate clearances – and to make this information available online via the library catalogue. Time was then spent with the student group explaining the initiative and supporting them throughout the pilot scheme. On completion of the pilot exercise, an evaluation and feedback session was arranged. Feedback was so positive that the scheme has now been extended to cover all units of the healthcare course. The last word on this highly successful teamwork initiative should rightly come from the college, which commented:

> We feel that we are ALL winners – our students, colleagues, library staff, Elmwood College and the library profession. As a profession librarians are not traditionally given to broadcasting their successes; we didn't set out to submit an entry for an award, but achieving one has certainly been a huge motivator.

As a postscript, Elmwood's idea of 'rovering' has been adopted by a number of higher education and further education libraries in the UK. Indeed, the 2010 CILIP professional development programme includes a session on roving with purpose in FE/HE libraries, which has been advertised as follows:

> Roving [or floor walking] has recently been adopted by a number of library and information services. The process helps library services to

become more proactive and provides point of use assistance to users wherever they are. Libraries who have adopted roving have found that it increases user and staff satisfaction, helps to reduce problems with negative behaviour and assists the 'hidden customer', i.e. those who may be reluctant to leave their work space or hesitant to ask for help... (CILIP, 2009)

Case study: Your sins will find you out...

A popular social networking site recently screened an extremely gross example of what can happen when low-paid, badly-motivated employees become terminally bored with their jobs. These two imaginatively-challenged and ultimately self-destructive individuals were employed by a major national pizza-delivery chain. While unsupervised in the back-room food preparation area, they filmed themselves doing things to the pizza ingredients which are best left to the imagination. Not content with this as-yet private 'gross-out' activity, they then thought it would be a good idea to screen their disturbing performance on YouTube. Not surprisingly, word got back to the company, and they were sacked on the spot. As if that was not a sufficiently hard lesson, warrants were also issued for their arrest.

Lessons learned

- Establish a working environment in which employees feel valued and respected, and are appropriately rewarded for their work, and you are unlikely to experience such massive damage to your 'brand' as this company undoubtedly suffered.

- Treat people like drones, and put them into a boring, repetitive production line where they feel undervalued, are poorly paid, and have little or no opportunity to express themselves in a positive way, and it should come as no surprise if they develop such negative feelings towards their employer that they may even resort to sabotage or worse.

- Despite the best intentions of any organisation, it is possible that some asocial individuals may still slip through the recruitment and training process, and end up as an employee. If you are unfortunate enough for this to happen in your organisation, just make sure that your disciplinary processes are sufficiently robust to enable you to weed out the dross at the earliest opportunity.

- Regularly check such social networks to see what people (particularly employees) are saying about your own company or organisation. Also make sure that your staff are fully aware of the power of such media, and about the potential damage (or even benefit) that such sites can deliver. The pizza horror movie had almost one million 'hits' in its relatively short life on YouTube.

- If you do experience bad press on such a site, be prepared to quickly make use of the same site to respond positively and at least minimise the damage. Don't just leave it to fester.

Further reading

Adair, J. (2004) *Concise Adair on Teambuilding and Motivation*, Sterling, VA: Throgood.

Ankarlo, L. (1998) *9 Traits of Highly Successful Work Teams*, Boulder, CO: Career Track Inc.

Barclay, C. (2009) 'Winners all round', *Information Scotland* 7(1), available at: *http://www.slainte.org.uk/publications/serials/infoscot/vol7%281%29/vol7%281%29article3.htm* (accessed 27 October 2009).

CILIP (2009) 'Roving with purpose HE/FE libraries', available at: *http://www.cilip.org.uk/jobs-careers/training/pages/roving-with-purpose-he-fe-libraries.aspx*.

Fleming, I. (2004) *The Teamworking Pocketbook*, Alresford: Management Pocketbooks.

Tuckman, B. (1965) 'Developmental sequence in small groups', *Psychological Bulletin* 63 (6): 384–99.

12

What are we good at, and what is our future? Action planning

Hide not your talents – they for use were made
What's a sundial in the shade?
(Benjamin Franklin)

The toughest thing about success is that you've got to keep on being a success. (Irving Berlin)

Many in the younger generations would prefer to surf the internet from the comfort of their home or expend their disposable income on the luxury of new entertainment items from hip stores rather than setting foot in a library ... have no idea ... that public libraries might be trying to foster a more welcoming image. (C. A. Gardner)

Aims

The aims of this chapter are as follows:

- to celebrate success and take pride in achievements;
- to actively share information about team successes;
- to make a commitment to improving customer service skills.

To assist with planning, Table 12.1 presents a suggested session plan.

Table 12.1 What are we good at? Action planning

Session	Aims	Content	Methods	Aids	Time (mins)
What are we good at?	To celebrate success and take pride in achievements	Introduction	T		5
		You are welcome to us!	A	F/C	15
		What motivates you?	A		5
	To actively share information about team successes	What are we good at?	A	F/C	15
Action planning	To make a commitment to improving customer service skills	Action planning	A	H/O	10
		My support network		F/C	10
Approx. total time (mins)					60

*A, activity (participants); F/C, flipchart; H/O, handout; P/I, Post-it notes; T, talk (facilitator)

Background

In Chapter 9, on confidence and assertiveness, we asked if you were able to accept compliments graciously. How often do you stop and give yourself a pat on the back for a job well done? When we accomplish something worthwhile, we deserve recognition.

Even if we don't always get positive feedback from others, we can and should give it to ourselves. It is easier to complain than to praise, and sometimes we can find it difficult to recognise and accept our successes. Many cultures tend to discourage people from 'boasting' about achievements. This chapter is giving you an opportunity to do just that.

To acknowledge a good job well done, it is important to consider what you are doing well and what you have accomplished. To make appreciation truly meaningful, it is worth celebrating success. We plod away each and every day, and celebrating helps us to keep going on the continuous quality journey. Consider the analogy of filling up your car with petrol in celebration of the miles covered and in preparation for the miles yet to be tackled. In a way, celebrating past successes is preparatory for the future.

When researching for an earlier book, we were struck by how many library users, in this case researchers, valued:

> the atmosphere, a sanctuary from the telephone and office-sharing colleagues where one may browse and discover materials by serendipity. The 'wow' factor of a large research library as an 'icon', something to be proud of, and an institutional asset needs to be capitalised upon in any marketing strategy. (Gannon-Leary et al., 2008: 6)

Imagine if a visitor from another organisation asked you what the most interesting things about your service were, and what you were most proud of. How would you answer? Would all members of staff give the same answer? What are the salient talking points about your service? Is there a bookmark, brochure or webpage that highlights these?

Hilyard (2007) describes how, in the staff room of her public library, she would on a fortnightly basis pose a new question/statement for staff to respond to using Post-it® notes. These could include such questions as 'What (positive) comments do you hear customers making about our branch?' and such statements as 'Pat your co-workers on the back – tell us what you've seen them doing well'. This is a nice way to encourage all staff to celebrate successes.

Aim 1: To celebrate success and take pride in achievements

You are welcome to us!

In this activity, participants are asked to consider the production of a 'welcome pack' for new members of their service team/section.

The activity involves listing what they would include to help orient and integrate a new recruit into the team. Remember that you want to give a positive picture, so consider what team/section successes you would want to share with the recruit.

The following list was produced by a team doing this activity:

- background to/history of the section;
- case studies/success stories;
- hierarchy diagrams with (smiling) photographs;
- how we got where we are;
- introduction to the team members and their roles and skills;
- map/plan of section;
- meet our customers (including user feedback);
- our unique selling point (e.g. special rare book collection);
- pack to have team/section logo;
- vision/mission statement;
- where we would like to be – positioning paper.

Your participants may come up with a different or even better list, but what is important is that they consider the inclusion of customer information in the pack. After all, most of this manual has been discussing customers as they are an integral part of your team. They are your raison d'être and should be involved up front.

What motivates you?

Give participants a few minutes to work individually and identify their top three motivators at work. Depending on the group dynamics and how the session is working, facilitators may wish to ask individual participants to share one of their motivators with the group. Don't make anyone feel uncomfortable about this – it may be preferable to seek volunteers rather than going round the group.

Some typical motivators include:

- bonus or award;
- customer gratitude (letters/testimonials);
- feeling valued by the organisation;
- good appraisal or peer review;
- pay day;
- praise from a colleague;
- pride in a job well done;

- promotion opportunities;
- recognition by line manager;
- sense of achievement;
- working in a dynamic team.

As part of this activity, facilitators can ask participants to consider what they have done in the past week that they are especially good at. They could also consider a positive attribute or characteristic that they believe they possess, which contributes positively to their customer service role. They don't have to share these with the group but may find them useful in subsequent activities.

Aim 2: To actively share information about team successes

What are we good at?

Split the participants into teams/sections for this activity if possible. Give them a flipchart and ask them to be as positive as possible in listing what their section/team is good at.

At the end of the exercise, consider what you could do to recognise the good things that have been identified and to reward performance. This could be something as simple as buying cream cakes for the team or going out for a celebratory meal. It doesn't have to involve food but, at this stage, the facilitators might want to hand round some fun-size candy bars or similar – have some fruit for those on special diets.

Aim 3: To make a commitment to improving customer service skills

Action planning

We are moving towards the end of the training and would like facilitator(s) and participants to think over the material covered and to reflect on:

- what they feel they have learned about dealing with customers;
- what have they learned about themselves and their team/section;
- how they might apply what they have learned.

To make a commitment to improving their customer service skills, we suggest that that participants design an action plan of specific targets to help them accomplish this overall goal.

Action planning involves:

- identifying and defining as clearly as possible what is happening *now* – the present state;

- developing a clear vision of the future and where we would like to be – our desired state;

- designing appropriate strategies to manage the transition between the two – a change of state.

If any step is missed out, the action plan will be weakened.

All the steps needs to be approached with equal priority and with personal strengths – both inspiring vision and an accurate grasp of current reality are required.

Individual action plans should show the present state (what I do well now) and the desired state (what I will do better). Goals should be numbered in the order of priority.

My support network

Support is vital to determine how well we are doing and to take plans forward. Support is also important for our health. It helps in stress reduction and in coping with transitions. It is important for our growth, and for building our confidence and competence.

Each of us has our own network of people from whom we receive, and to whom we give, support. These people may be mentors, colleagues, friends or family. They help by actively listening to us and by empathising/understanding. They show us respect and regard us in a positive light. They give us emotional support as well as practical assistance.

Give the participants some time for self-assessment using the following prompts:

- Take stock of the people in your support network.

- Assess the types of support they give you.

- Assess your satisfaction level (for each person).

- Identify changes/additions to your support network.

- Consider how you might make changes yourself and develop your own networking/support skills.

Having considered these points, participants can pursue any of a number of approaches. They may feel they have a support network within the training group. In this case, they may wish to agree to contact a partner within the group in two month's time to check on their progress as regards their action plans. Alternatively, they may prefer to mail their action plans to one of the facilitators and then get in touch two months later to see how much they have achieved. It depends on the group dynamics.

Exemplar: A vision of the future at Aarhus Public Library, Denmark

Since the early 1990s, Aarhus Public Library has been developing its digital services. The more work it did, the more it recognised the links between this digital work and the more general work of enhancing the library as a space with a variety of IT-based support. This led the library to formulate a vision of the 'intelligent' library space.

This vision, encompassing such initiatives as the info column, info galleria, digital floor and radio-frequency ID book phones, represented the desire to create a physical and experiential learning environment in which the user could navigate interactively to digital content. It was also driven by a strong belief in the need to be proactive in relation to the fast movement of 'pervasive and ubiquitous' computing – the fact that computer-based intelligence is increasingly embedded in the artefacts surrounding us in our daily life.

Below, we describe some of the initiatives realised as part of Aarhus Public Library's vision of intelligent physical space:

- *Website*: The original, static webpages have been replaced with content management systems. The library's new dynamic and interactive website gives access to a variety of services, including personalised profile, e-mail notifications on holds and overdue books, web payment of fees and fines, notification before loans expire, subscribed personalised subject list on newly purchased media, business information, surveys and polls, virtual tours and maps, RSS feeds and SMS services.

- *OPAC*: Online public access catalogues have developed significantly since the turn of the century. Web-service technology has made it possible to embed elements from other web-based data sources in the catalogue, e.g. images of copyright-cleared book front-pages, systems based on collaborative filtering, and statistical data on loan patterns have all been developed to exploit the 'wisdom of crowds' in creating recommendation facilities similar to the well-known recommendations on commercial websites such as Amazon. Features for customising and personalising the OPAC are in the pipeline, whereby the user can track their own loans, holds and possible fines for overdue material.

- *Mobile portals*: This represents a relatively new service, where the library gives access to a range of services for internet-enabled mobile phones. The services range from information on opening hours and the status of borrowed materials, fees and fines, to news on programmes. There are also SMS services providing reading suggestions and recommendations, and facilities to place orders and holds on desired books. The growth of broadband-connected mobile devices in the market has provided the necessary infrastructure, and the potential for mobile access to library services can hardly be overestimated. There is little doubt that new services pushing content will emerge shortly, such as samples, citations and quotations from new literature, young authors' poetry, and Q&A services.

- *Digital content*: Today, digital content includes e-texts, e-books, e-zines, music, photos, images, film and audio-books that are directly available through download or down-loan services. Download allows the user permanent use of the e-source, while down-loan provides the user with time-limited access to digital media managed by through digital rights management systems. An increasing number of audio-books in MP3 format are available through the library OPAC. When performing a search, the user gets a result showing books in the library, e-books for immediate download, and audio books in MP3 format for down-loan.

- *Bibliotek.dk*: This free collaborative web-based search and ordering facility (*http://bibliotek.dk*) makes it possible for a user anywhere in Denmark to have physical media, books, magazines, CDs, DVDs, delivered from any library in the country to a library in his or her neighbourhood.

- *Net libraries*: At present, there are 19 net libraries in operation in Denmark, including:

  - Biblioteksvagten (*http://www.biblioteksvagten.dk*) – an online question and answering service operated by librarians from 71 public and research libraries.

  - Libraries Net Music (*https://www.netmusik.dk*) – not by definition a net library, but rather a library service that allows registered users access to down-loan MP3 files from a selection of more than a million music tracks. After a loan period of one or seven days, the music piece will erase itself, unless the user chooses to buy it.

- A children's portal has undergone total reconstruction and was re-launched in late 2009.

- Ask Olivia (*http://www.spoergolivia.dk*) – a question and answer service for children, which presents various possibilities for interaction including games and reading recommendations.

- Litteratursiden (*http://www.litteratursiden.dk*) – a portal promoting contemporary Danish and foreign fiction. The main editor is based in Aarhus Public Library, but the consortium consists of public libraries from 79 municipalities. All participating libraries perform some sort of production work for the site. The portal includes an e-zine with e-mail notification for more than 3,000 subscribers; book clubs; advice; recommendations; articles; a database on contemporary Danish authors including video and audio clips, biographies and bibliographies; opportunity for placing holds and requisitions through bibliotek.dk; and facilities for the participating libraries to use web service technologies to automatically embed content, such as recommendations, in their own OPACs. The site has partnered with a Danish national public service television broadcasting company and has 3.6 million individual visits annually – a very high usage rate relative to the population of Denmark.

Aarhus Public Library worked in close cooperation with the Alexandra Institute and ISIS Kathrinebjerg, the research and development departments of Aarhus University, as well as with private partners. The i-floor was also implemented at some public sector schools in Aarhus, labelled as the 'knowledge well'.

Feedback on the scheme has been very positive, and has directly influenced the way the library thinks about development. The library actively engages its customers, and the phrase 'user-driven innovation' is very much the reality. The library has published an accessible user guide, which clearly describes user involvement for libraries (see *http://presentations .aakb.dk/publikationer/the_librarys_voice_eng.pdf*).

The info-galleria are now being rolled out in more than 20 municipal public libraries in Denmark, as well as in other local institutions in Aarhus and municipal citizens' services and sport and leisure public services. The key to success is the software that allows both centralised and decentralised editing of content, and the organisations behind the creation of content, where many libraries work together and divide the tasks.

Further development is planned, targeted towards completing the new main library 'urban media space' by 2014 (see *http://www.thefindbuzz .com/tag/urban+media+space*).

For further information on this initiative, see Sidsel Bech-Petersen's article, 'The mash-up library' (*http://www.aakb.dk/graphics/user/HB/Ledelse per cent20og per cent20konsulenter/mashuplibrary.pdf*) or the video about the ideas and rationale (*http://www.youtube.com/watch?v=TpFO_L_jA1c*).

Aarhus Public Library is also developing is the idea of the 'library as a universe'. It has directly engaged young customers as 'mindspotters', exploiting their networks and competences to build totally new services and experiences both inside and outside the library. For more on this development project, see the video (*http://www.youtube.com/watch? v=ixsOLvLSARg*) and the report (*http://www.aakb.dk/graphics/portal/ young/Refleksionsrapporter/mindspot_rapport_eng_web.pdf*).

Exemplar: The 24-hour media vending machine at Newcastle City Library

At a time when libraries both locally and nationally are experiencing a significant increase in customers, Newcastle City Council's forward-thinking approach aims to capitalise on this renewed interest by transforming the way library services are delivered.

Opened to the public on 7 June 2009, Newcastle City Library occupies a new, six-floor building that includes a 185-seat performance space, meeting rooms and crèche facilities. This state-of-the-art library operates on a fully self-service basis, enabling staff to devote more time to providing more focused help and advice to customers.

The library has a 24-hour vending machine that opens onto the street and holds up to 400 books, CDs and DVDs. Items can also be returned on a 24-hour basis, regardless of opening times.

The vending machine looks rather like a large cash machine and provides access to books, audio-books, and DVDs on a 24/7 basis. Customers use a touch-screen to choose from a variety of available media. Access is via a card-reader, which first verifies user details and then supplies the requested items. Return transactions are just as easy. Moreover, the returned item is then immediately available for reissue. The machine is directly linked to the main library computer system and provides real-time updates on both customer and transaction details. An additional advantage to the 24/7 availability is that it has the potential to draw in new customers who may not be able to access library services during normal opening hours.

Exemplar: ImaginOn – a joint venture between Charlotte Public Library and the Children's Theatre of Charlotte, NC

In Charlotte, North Carolina, the Charlotte Public Library and the Children's Theatre of Charlotte were running out of space. The directors of the two institutions recognised that they shared not only a problem, but also a mission: bringing stories to life. As such, they agreed that to meet the growing needs of both organisations, it would make sense to consider creating a new, shared facility. This new facility would not just be a combined library/theatre – they imagined a new type of facility, and an original approach to education, learning and the arts. Thus, in 1997, the seed of 'ImaginOn' was sown, its mission being to 'bring stories to life through extraordinary experiences that challenge, inspire, and excite young minds'.

The new facility opened in October 2005, with the Story Lab very much the core of this imaginative project. Children are drawn to its huge Story Jar (meant to represent the millions of stories in the world), and to the old records, umbrellas and shoes dangling from the mobile hanging above.

Children visiting the Story Lab quickly settle into individual workstations (called Tale Spinners) or the pod-like arrangements of computers (called Team Machines) scattered throughout the room. Even the computers themselves are designed to enhance the 'magical' effect for their young users. No standard, grey or buff machines here, but purples and yellows, with fantastic spiralling turrets and pipes leading off to unknown places.

The students use software that guides them through the story-writing process, and challenges them to use their imagination in exciting flights of fancy. When they are finished, they can 'add' their stories to the Story Jar or, if they have a library card, they can revise them later at home or school.

The children who have chosen the Team Machine work with software that helps them create a theatrical scene. As they invent the storyline, design the set and fashion the costumes, they interact excitedly. It can be a noisy process.

From the Story Lab, a ramp curves upward toward the upper level, leading to Tech Central – an installation of 40 computers for 'tweens'. Staffed by a five-member technology education team, Tech Central provides software for learning and recreation, as well as internet access for those with parental permission. What is unique about Tech Central is its educational mission – the staff are not there simply to monitor children, but also to teach them. An adjacent computer classroom with 15 workstations provides an opportunity for children and teens to learn not just library research and database searching, but a whole variety of computer-based programs and tools appropriate to their age and experience. Opportunities for hands-on learning are an essential part of ImaginOn's design. There are four other classrooms – to be used for rehearsals or workshops with budding playwrights, as well as studios for dance and art classes. An artist-in-residence would fit perfectly into ImaginOn's vision.

The ramp finally ends at the Teen Loft, a nearly 4,000-square-foot space with its own distinct look and feel. Oversized booths provide space for teens to work together – or just to meet friends and to talk. Huge easy chairs beg for readers to curl up in them. A media area, all metal and glass, feels more like an upmarket coffee bar.

Studio-I, adjacent to the Loft, is one of ImaginOn's most ambitious innovations. Using blue-screen technology, this 1,225-square-foot studio gives teens the opportunity to produce live-action and animated videos, using the latest techniques, such as stop-motion, clay and two-dimensional animation. Studio-I also includes three workstations, and with the help of the ed-tech team, fledgling video artists can learn how to shoot, edit and mix sound. While Studio-I complements ImaginOn's storytelling mission, it is radical for a library to so actively embrace the artistically creative process – as opposed to just collection – in a medium that isn't just text. Studio-I finally gives teens, huge consumers of video content, an opportunity to create and express through video.

The manager of the Teen Loft sums up the ethos of this imaginative and highly successful project: 'traditional libraries reach traditional users. Non-traditional libraries reach everybody'.

Feedback has been very positive, and the facility is highly valued as a community resource. Strong links have been made with local schools, and ImaginOn is heavily booked for summer camps in particular.

Future plans include further development of community programmes and partnerships. Classes and workshops will be offered, focused on both literary and performing arts. One area in which there is particular interest is in the potential for adapting children's literature for theatrical performance.

For further information, see Kenney (2005).

Further reading

Gannon-Leary, P., Bent, M. and Webb, J. (2008) 'A destination or a place of last resort: The research library of the future, its users and its librarians', *Library and Information Research* 32(10): 3–14.

Gardner, C. A. (2005) 'The importance of customer service', *Virginia Libraries* 51(4): 2–4.

Hilyard, N. B. (2007) 'Making changes and staying happy', *Public Libraries* 46(3): 17–24

Kenney, B. (2005) 'Imagine this'. *School Library Journal* 51(12): 52–5.

Wrapping it up

In three words, I can sum up everything I have learned about life.
It goes on... (Robert Frost)

Concluding remarks

Before asking the participants for feedback on the course, it is worth
giving a repeat synopsis of the course and its aims, and to quickly review
the subjects covered and the intended learning outcomes. It may be worth
distributing the following list to participants as an aide-memoire to take
away with them. Certainly, it forms a useful point of reference for longer-
term reflection on the key issues of the course. No tabular session plan is
included here, but as a rough guide, the delivery of a short synopsis, and
the circulation of feedback forms should take no more than about 20
minutes.

- *What is customer service?*
  - Defining quality customer service
  - Characterising excellent customer service
  - Understanding the need for enthusiasm and a positive attitude
    towards customer service
  - Seeing more opportunities to improve customer service
  - Increasing awareness of how and why excellent customer service
    can produce outstanding results
  - Highlighting the customer service chain and the influence that
    internal service can have on external service delivery
- *Who are our customers? The customer service chain*
  - Determining customer needs

- Being aware of stated and unstated needs in the customer service transaction so that they can offer value-added
- Understanding why meeting their needs keeps customers coming back

- *Communication*
  - Establishing a rapport with customers – those important first impressions
  - Body language and the subtle messages we send to, and receive from, our customers
  - Practical knowledge of customer service concepts and practices developing communication skills
  - Clarifying terminology
  - Defining and applying the most appropriate communication style for dealing effectively with diverse customers

- *Questioning and active listening*
  - The power of questions
  - Listening: the key 'under-taught' skill in dealing with customers
  - Establishing working relationships with customers

- *Handling complaints*
  - A chance to evaluate some of your present customer service strategies
  - How to turn customer complaints into customer service opportunities
  - Developing skills to deal with customer complaints

- *Dealing with challenging situations*
  - How to avoid attitudes and behaviour that drive customers away
  - Confidence and developing skills to resolve customer conflict
  - Identifying ways of staying stress-free and able to calm upset/ emotional customers
  - Increasing confidence in abilities to manage difficult situations

- *Life positions and the OK Corral: being more confident and assertive*
  - Assertiveness and handling those extra difficult situations
  - Understanding influencing styles and adapting approaches to suit diverse customers
  - Developing and implementing win-win customer service strategies

- *Suggestions for improvement*
  - Benefiting the organisation by having more empowered frontline service staff with a direct and positive impact on customer satisfaction

- Challenging the way things have been done in the past and thinking about change
- Identifying critical areas of service weakness and therefore opportunities to improve service performance
- Considering a range of customer research approaches for identifying and establishing customer needs and expectations
- Developing effective customer satisfaction feedback mechanisms appropriate to your organisation

- *Teambuilding*
  - Helping participants become important team members, and more energised and focused
  - Fostering appreciation of how good teamwork and support are vital to customer service
  - Promoting staff for customer service and not for 'boss watching'

- *What are we good at, and what is our future? Action planning*
  - Developing a range of proactive strategies for exceeding customer expectations
  - Using innovation and creativity to develop new ways to exceed customer expectations
  - Laying foundations for excellence in customer service
  - Establishing and maintaining a culture of continuous improvement

Feedback

At the end of the course, the facilitators can give out feedback sheets for the participants. These may be produced by your own organisation or you may wish to devise your own. If you do this, remember what we said previously about feedback. We have included a version of our own feedback sheet which you may wish to use (or critique – we are not perfect either!). You might just want to pose the following simple, non-directive statements:

- What I liked most about the course was...
- What I liked least about the course was...
- What I would change about the course is...

If you wish to obtain oral feedback, consider asking the participants what their most significant learning was. Each participant should respond individually after they have had a few moments to think about this. They could write their thoughts down before replying – at this stage they should feel able to articulate their opinions freely. Depending on the time available, all or some of the following additional questions could be asked:

- What have you learned are your most important needs?
- What are the next small steps you will take?
- To what extent do you feel the goal, objectives, outputs and outcomes of the course have been achieved?
- To what extent do your expectations on registering for the course correlate with the above?
- Do you as a group want to make a statement? (If so, it must be realistic and doable.)
- If you were to run a similar course, what would you do differently in terms of both content and process?

Remember to thank the participants when you say goodbye!

Course evaluation form

Course: Title/date

Presented by: Organisation/facilitator

Thank you for attending this course. Please fill in the evaluation form below – your feedback will help us improve our future programmes.

1. *Your name and e-mail address (optional)*:
2. *Were the course aims made clear to you in advance (e.g. through the invitation)?*
   - Not clear
   - Somewhat clear
   - Very clear
3. *How useful did you find the course overall?*
   - Not useful
   - Somewhat useful
   - Very useful

4. *How satisfied were you with the facilitator/facilitator?*
   - Not satisfied
   - Somewhat satisfied
   - Very satisfied

5. *How satisfied were you with the handouts?*
   - Not satisfied
   - Somewhat satisfied
   - Very satisfied

6. *How did you find the pace of the course?*
   - Too slow
   - About right
   - Too fast

7. *How did you find the length of the course?*
   - Too short
   - About right
   - Too long

8. *How satisfied were you with the organisation of the course?*
   - Not satisfied
   - Somewhat satisfied
   - Very satisfied

9. *Please use this space for any other comments and suggestions for improvement*

Thank you for your help! Please return your forms to your facilitator.

Conclusion

Four short words sum up what has lifted most successful individuals above the crowd: 'a little bit more'. They did all that was expected of them, and a little bit more. (A. Lou Vickery)

Plenary

You have now seen how the course could be run in a variety of formats, over one or two days, either consecutive or delivered over subsequent weeks. It can also be tailored to the specific needs of the participants, depending on whether they are work teams or cross-functional staff. As the facilitators grow more confident, they will see how they can adopt a pick-and-mix approach to the material. You will find that many of the exercises are work-related, drawing on the participants' knowledge and experience so that, in effect, you and the participants can 'self-customise' the contents and in the process develop insights and perceptions readily applicable to real-life situations.

We hope that the training techniques you have derived from this manual have helped participants to review and evaluate the customer care they currently provide, to develop skills and strategies to further improve, to become more resourceful, and to develop action plans for greater excellence that exceeds customers' expectations.

Some final words...

You know you have had an effective course when:

- The right people were
  - present;

- prepared;
- participating.

- Information was shared and processed appropriately.
- Objectives and expectations were met.
- Participants felt a sense of accomplishment.
- Action plans were set with responsibilities assigned.
- Enough time was allocated to cover all the items on the agenda.
- The course started and ended on time.

Index

Breinigsville, PA USA
24 March 2010
234856BV00003B/2/P